# 24:50

# 50 DAYS OF REFLECTION

## A VISUAL DEVOTIONAL BOOK

Noella Kazadi

# CONTENTS

❧ I ❧

# FOREWORD

Putting this book together was quite an interesting journey to say the least; this has been over two years in the making. As you will realise from reading this, life can be a very emotional rollercoaster, but the most gratifying feeling was the decision I made to retell it in its rawest form. Enjoy!

# ACKNOWLEDGEMENTS

There are many people that have been a huge part of this book coming to life. I would like to extend my heartfelt gratitude to each and every person. However, this book is dedicated to my grandmother, Melanie Longo, a rare creation with a heart of gold. You have raised generations of God-fearing men and women; you will forever be known for your strong and selfless character. I love you Mama Nkambo, this one is for you.

# INTRODUCTION

❧ I ❧

To God be all the glory, honour and power for giving me the inspiration to voice my pain, joy and journey. One day I was sitting down at home; I was not having a very good day. Something was telling me, *"Write how you feel."* I took my laptop out and wrote the first chapter. I remember feeling as though a weight was lifted off my heart and that is how the journey of this book commenced. As you will gather from reading the book, this was not written in 50 consecutive days. I gave up too many times to count, I felt inadequate far more times than I can recall, yet because God had given me the vision to tell this story, he was able to carry me through. This book is both the combination of my life experience and observations of the journeys of others. I can shamelessly say that I did not write this book because I am an expert, nor was it written in retrospect. I am still on the journey to growth, self-love and faith. I pray that as you read this book, you laugh, reflect and take action too. I did not study English literature or creative writing at university, I simply believed in God's vision for this book. At this point, there is one thing left to say; grab a cup of tea, sit back and enjoy the ride.

God bless.

# ONE

*"For we were saved in this hope, but hope that is seen is not hope, for why does one still hope for what he sees?"*
**Romans 8:24**

Today I am feeling hopeful that I can give more in this life. Hopeful that I will be able to contribute my abilities to the progression of this world. I hope that I will be able to fight the good fight of faith.

For a while now, things have not been going the way I wanted them to. Feelings of inadequacy fill my mind, and I don't know what to do about it. I was beginning to accept my ongoing problems. This morning I had somewhat of an epiphany about wants and needs, and everything changed. Until this morning, I had assumed there was a difference between them, but the truth soon became clear.

I may want to structure my life in a particular way, but I might also shadow that want with my lack of motivation. Imagine being in a desert with no food, no water, no way out, and no hope. In such a situation you would have two options: You could either accept the unlikelihood of your survival, or you could try your best to survive. In that situation, the *need* to survive would be more important than the *want* to give up.

It is imperative that you treat hope like a need instead of a want. You will do everything in your power to make sure nothing kills nor deters your attention from your hope. As I said earlier, today I am feeling hopeful because I was entrenched in my worry and allowed life to pass me by. I looked at my phone, I went on Facebook and Instagram, I watched movies, I went on WhatsApp and made phone calls. I managed to do all the above in one day repeatedly, but I still felt sorry for myself, yet failed to do anything about it; I failed to make my life count.

Then I heard a preacher say that the only thing that is not in your control is time. You may decide to slow down, stop, visit Facebook or watch movies; it is your choice. I am 23 years old. I thought to myself, *I have plenty of time.*

Then an inner voice said to me, *Do you remember when you were 16?*

I responded, *I remember being sixteen as though it was yesterday.*

My inner voice replied, *I rest my case.*

Seven years ago, I was 16, but I allowed circumstances of life to worry me and waste my time because I assumed I had plenty of it. Yet here I am again, ready to let another seven years pass by for the same reason.

The true question is: What are you going to do with the hope you have today?

# I WANT HOPE - I NEED HOPE.

# TWO

❧ I ❧

### *"We can complain because rose bushes have thorns, or rejoice because thorn bushes have roses."*
**Abraham Lincoln**

Today I am thoughtful. I am thinking about what I have accomplished in life and how much I still want to pursue. There are times when I am frustrated with myself because things are not going according to plan. I sigh inwardly, and on occasion sigh outwardly too.

I tend to believe that I could do more if I had more time to achieve my goals. I feel like I must work twice as hard to prove myself to people and to fulfil my ambitions.

Although I am grateful for everything the Lord has done in my life, my feelings of inadequacy discourage me at times. This happens when I allow my mind to compare me to people within my age group.

A comparison is not inherently bad. In fact, I would argue that it can be both great and terrible. What matters is the function the comparison has in our everyday living. You will find yourself using comparison to undermine your efforts, self-esteem, and progress. In many instances, you'll find that the criticism that comes from these comparisons are unjustified, yet the danger of unfairly judging yourself remains. Instead I ask myself, *What can I do to improve my efforts to achieve future goals, and how would this inspire me?*

You should never use the excuse 'if I have more, I can achieve more', because that is the attitude of excuse-giving people. A person who truly wants something will use every tool in their possession to make greatness happen; they even find methods of acquiring more tools or skills when necessary. No great man or woman in this world considered their poverty as an adequate excuse to give up. Use what you have, and who you have, to cook an amazing dish of greatness.

The first fan of your work, your achievements, and your journey must be YOU. We allow our thoughts to eat us up because we become concerned with who we will disappoint and the expectations that people have of us. When we feel that our current life is not quite reflecting people's expectations, we end up in a state of negative thinking. Although this may sound highly cliché, it is still highly important that you always try to think positively, even if your current position or situation makes it difficult to do so. I personally believe that positive thinking is a big step towards finding a solution to your problem, and it also brings you a step closer to reaching your goals.

# CAN YOU SEE THE BIGGER PICTURE?

# THREE

*"Sometimes you have to accept that you are not strong enough today; that may be the only way for you to get stronger tomorrow."*
**Noella Kazadi**

oday I woke up feeling fed-up. I am fed-up with life. I have so many things going on through my mind, but no answers or solutions for any of them. Have you ever found yourself in a place where not only do you not know how you got there, but you also don't know how to get out? You literally feel stuck. That is my very feeling today. I ask myself, *Am I the only person that goes through this, or does everyone else also go through it too?* The hardest thing for me to do today was to get out of my bed. In my mind I know exactly what to do. I know that God is able; however, in all honesty, today I am just not feeling him near my situation.

I was trying to ask myself, *Is it something I did? Surely, it must be me?* The more I asked myself questions that I did not have answers to, the more frustrated and overwhelmed I felt. It is as though I have something huge stuck in my throat and this thing is stopping my breathing; it is completely suffocating me. But I have not figured out a way to remove it from my throat without totally stopping breathing, so I have to live with it until I figure out a way to separate the two and keep myself alive.

There are many times in your life you might have felt the way I feel today, and I know it is the hardest thing to put into words. You can try to explain it to people, yet you may still feel as though even the closest people to you don't quite understand your exact sentiment. I tend to go into a state of isolation. I will either completely disappear from the face of the earth, hide in my room for days, or put on a tough face and be around people without showing my true emotions. One of the things I hate is pity. Have you ever confided in somebody, and right after they have this gloomy face and ask you, "Are you okay?" Some find comfort through this. I, on the other hand, find that this question makes me more disheartened. Therefore, to spare myself the emotional rollercoaster, I just keep it in. Does the above solve anything? Absolutely not. I do believe that being honest about certain habits and coping mechanisms can help you make a change.

**THERE ARE OVER 7 BILLION PEOPLE, BUT THE WORLD CAN BE SUCH A LONELY PLACE.**

# FOUR

❧ I ❧

*"Nothing great will ever be achieved without great men, and men are great only if they are determined to be so."*
**Charles de Gaulle**

Today I woke up feeling determined. I must push myself to believe that hard work does pay off, and if you just keep pushing and keep at it even when times get hard, you're bound to start retrieving some results. Even if these results are only minimal today, even if these results are not your end goal, you must start somewhere. Be proud of the work that you put in daily, be proud of the person you are becoming, because soon enough everything will start falling into place.

Have you ever run a race? I am sure we all have, at least in school at some point. When the race starts, you find that it is almost effortless, and some people even start to speed up at the beginning (I am guilty of this). However, at some point you start to feel your heart beat rapidly, your feet heavier. You begin to see the ground in motion, the sky and your head spinning at the same time. Getting to the finish line becomes much harder than you anticipated. It seems that the easiest option is to give up, drink water, grab a burger and go to sleep.

The most rewarding option, however, is to ignore the temporary suffering and get to the finish line. Although everything within you will be telling you to stop or at least slowdown, you must find the drive to keep pushing until you reach the finish line.

That is how you must view life on certain days; you need an unwavering desire to win. Remember, it is not a race against anyone but rather a race against yourself and a race against time. If you lose, you only let yourself down. Today I challenge you to not be a quitter or a coward. I challenge you to be determined and do something amazing. Even if it does not impress other people, know within yourself that it is one of your pending accomplishments, and you are a winner.

Today is not an easy day, but I will fight. I will prepare myself, and I refuse to quit because today I will motivate myself. I am reminded that I was created for a purpose. I know that today will never come back, so I am determined to make a choice to use this day wisely.

# AGAINST ALL ODDS...PUSH!

# FIVE

*"The secret of success is consistency of purpose."*
**Benjamin Disraeli**

Have you ever allowed situations and other things to pile up, not knowing where to repair the damage that has been caused to the extent that you decide to leave things a while longer? All it takes is one slipup to develop inconsistency. I have asked myself, *Is there truly any point in all the hard and miserable days? Is there a light to guide me out of these dark woods?* The more I thought about it, the less I did and the more I solidified my excuse.

The price of inconsistency is, of course, falling behind time; playing catch-up is worse than having achieved the given task at its rightful time because the process is extremely exhausting. Understand this, simpler is not always better. You can build yourself a brighter future and fully live your destiny, but you must find a reason to fight the right way.

Every day ask yourself, what is your cause? For some people it may be wanting a better life for their families, for others it may be wanting to prove all the doubters wrong. For some people, it may be simply wanting to obtain their goals. Whatever the reason is, you can decide what you need to tell yourself in order to keep pushing. The world we live in will not accept anything less. Imagine you have a babysitter, and on some days the babysitter is great. They look after your child, feed them, play with them and pretty much do everything the way you would. However, on other days they come late, they have a bad attitude, they neglect your baby and they don't change them or feed them. I am certain that any decent human being would fire that babysitter because it doesn't matter how good they can be; you don't want to put your baby at risk. Now imagine what you're doing to your destiny every time you decide to not commit to being consistent. It's your baby! Look after it diligently.

**COME ON, TRY AGAIN! TRY TODAY AS THOUGH YOU DIDN'T DO IT YESTERDAY.**

# SIX

*"I was a child that dreamt of putting on a cape and flying. I grew up and built a cape that could help me aim high."*
**Noella Kazadi**

❧  I  ❧

When I was younger, I used to dream and fill my mind and imagination of a perfect world, where there was peace and where I would achieve great things; it was a world without struggles or hardship. When I got a little older, I soon realised that such a world does not exist, so I built a wall of doubt. I chose to be realistic and not try to even dream nor imagine anything outside my circle. In this circle, teachers tell you the maximum capacity of your brain, your friends advise you of what is in your best interest, and your boss categorizes you in accordance to what he/she has observed. Therefore, you live your life abiding by these rules and you end up being nothing but mediocre, nothing but average. Nothing but another STATISTIC.

I realised that my childhood dream was the place I felt most confident because I could dream to be anything I wanted without feeling psychologically threatened or pressured to adhere to societal norms. I observed that I was at my strongest when I returned to that place of inner certainty. The only difference is simply knowing that it will not happen without a fight. The roads that I thought were straight may actually have some bends, some thorns and some puddles, but the destination is still the same. In my perfect childhood dream, I saw the world full of good people. I thought that if I wished everyone well, everyone must wish good onto me. That has proven to not be the case. In other words, I understood that just because you have the same dream does not automatically make you an appropriate candidate to go through this journey with me, because you may not have my best interests at heart.

You need to appreciate that you are your number one cheerleader on your success journey, and you ought to also be the number one critique of your mistakes. You won't always know whether the people cheering your dreams are doing it for the right reasons, or whether the people criticizing your work are highlighting your mistakes with good intentions. Once you have found your small inner circle, you will be at ease, but bear in mind that this may change as your vision grows, or rather as your dreams start to become a reality. Remember to think back to the child you were, the one who used to see possibilities in the future, but remain the adult who is not easily deceived by appearance.

# THE AMENDED AUTHENTIC CHILD'S VISION.

# SEVEN

❧ I ❧

*"Above all else, guard your heart with all diligence, for everything you do flows from it."*
**Proverbs 4:23**

Today I woke up thinking about the heart that God gives us and how much it can take until it cannot take any more. I woke up thinking about my own heart and how much I can take before I reach boiling point. I thought about all the trials and tribulations, disappointments, joys, sadness, surprises, heartaches and pains that a human being goes through each year. The truth is some people have it worse than others yet somehow find a way to fight through every stumbling block and still come out triumphant. It makes me wonder how strong a human heart truly is. It also validates how much it must be protected, constantly evaluated, cleansed and renewed.

This thought led me to reflect on the things which have come into my heart, the things that I have had to accept and the things that I must let go. Most importantly asking God to grant me understanding to know the difference. We don't sometimes comprehend how much our hearts have endured because we don't make time to evaluate what we take in and what we let out. Learn to let go of negative situations. I am not talking about the physical exercise of removing people from your circle; I am talking about actually sitting down and dealing with problems. I am talking about letting go of the negativity that is in your heart because it is possible for you to cut someone out and cut a situation out while allowing it or them to still occupy space within your heart. The more of these situations you have, the less space you will have to welcome positivity within your heart.

You are the master of your heart. God has prepared so many great things to come and inhabit your heart in order for you to be happy and fulfilled. I have discovered there is a major difference between your heart being happy and your heart being fulfilled. It is easy for someone to bring you temporary happiness, but in the long term you will see that you are not being fulfilled. On the other hand, please understand that true fulfilment generates happiness.

There will be times when we allow the negative energy to become part of us, and we do not even see nor are we willing to give a chance to real inner fulfillment. Your heart is big, your heart is strong, your heart can take a lot in and still survive. But, just because it can, does not mean it should. (*Selah*)

Everything we let in has a consequence, whether positive or negative. Make a decision to not force your heart to go through a lot of pain. Fight to protect your heart and pray that God may give you the fulfillment you require. If you allow your heart to constantly absorb negativity, the mind will also adjust. In other words, you begin to tell yourself, '*I cannot be more*', '*I cannot achieve more*', and '*this is what I deserve*'. You don't pay close attention to this, but sadly you have settled.

In the same manner you take time to wash daily (at least I hope so) and look after your health. Spend time to also wash your heart daily. You need to look after it, nourish it, build it and remove anything that threatens its health. The ability for the heart to get stronger or weaker lies in your hands. You will get hurt, you will laugh, you will cry, you will even hurt others, but all of this is just the cycle of life. Remember nonetheless, that you have a heart that was created to be fulfilled.

# THE UNCOVERED TREASURE.

# EIGHT

*"I wish there was a quote that could even begin to put into words who you were, I am still searching."*
**Noella Kazadi**

You've been heavily on my mind today. I have so much to tell you. You were the most wonderful, caring, gentle human being. Sometimes I think it is slightly unfair, slightly selfish that you do not allow me to speak to you. Even if you did, I am unable to. I have so much that I just want to pour out to you. You were the opposite of me; gentle, tolerant, kind and, above all, a King. Do you remember when I helped you build the farm in our house? I still can't believe that you built it from scratch. I remember we used to play a game where we would pretend to be in your army and you would be our commander telling us how soldiers behave. I remember going on a bike ride with you and I was at the back of the ride. We arrived at your friend's house, I don't quite remember what he offered you to eat, but you watched me until I asked you for some. To my surprise, you refused to give me any. I asked you why, and you said I must never beg, I must always wait patiently. Somehow, deep in my heart, I knew you understood me.

Do you remember when you found me playing with toy pots and I was pretending to cook? You laughed at me when I asked you if you wanted some food. You said, "Noella, you will never cook for me." I told you to wait because, *"One day, I will."* You should see me now. I can actually cook but you were right, I can never cook for you because you left me. Some days I miss you so much that it hurts. I feel that if I tell anyone, they would think I am crazy. They would think I was too young to remember you, but I know that you knew I loved you and still do. I hate the last conversation we had; you asked me, *"When are you going to come back and see me"?* I said, *"We will come and see you soon."* Then you said, *"You need to hurry up and see me before I die,"* and I laughed and said, *"You will not die before I see you."* But once again I was wrong. That was it for us.

I miss you so much today. Sometimes it hurts so much and I just want to pick up the phone and tell you all about it, but I can't do that. The way I remember me with you is the last time you saw me; I remembered me as your little girl. You always told me that I was strong, you reminded me of that every time I helped you build that farm. I don't always feel strong; sometimes I wish I could hear you remind me one more time that I am strong. I miss you, I miss you…I miss you.

Today has just been one of those days where I miss you. I know you don't know this because we didn't talk again, but the night before you died, your picture in our living room dropped right before my eyes. The next day, we got the news that you were gone, and all I could see in my head was the image of that picture falling down. Most days I am not sad because I know you went to a better place, but not today. Today I miss your smile. That heart-breaking news has taken a piece of my heart, and although time has passed, I can never ever stop loving you.

I saw your precious, beautiful, strong wife last year; she is a fighter. As soon as I saw her, I broke down in tears because the last time I saw her was with you. But this time she was alone.

If there's something you did right, you married a champion. I cannot put into words how precious she is. I hugged her and I know time doesn't stop, but I promise you it did then. I held her tightly as my mind went down memory lane. Can you believe I am much taller than her now? She is the most precious creation you could ever imagine. If I have half the heart she has, I know I will be fine.

I know you are in a better place, I know God took you to rest and he knows what he was doing. Oh, before I forget, you should have been here to see your son; you would have been so proud. Everything you believed in has come true. You should have seen him on that dance floor, celebrating his highest success in education, that night was all about him. Your hard work has come true, Commander. I know he misses you too, but believe me when I say you would be proud. I guess all that is left to say is, continue to rest in peace Papa Nkambo.

## KEEP SMILING, I LOVE YOU PAPA NKAMBO.

# NINE

*"Music expresses that which cannot be said and on which it is impossible to be silent."*
**Victor Hugo**

My thoughts? "No, not today." Music is powerful, it can take us back through time and we can feel what we felt. We can remember our conversations and we can even remember the weather on that day. Sometimes when you're in your darkest place, take your headset, find a quiet space, and blast out your music. We will not get into a debate about what you should listen to; however, for me there is nothing like a great worship song that just brings you to a place of peace. There will be days where you cannot even sing along to the words because your heart is too heavy. Your words end up sounding like a broken record and you're afraid that your next ones will come out with pain, anger or sadness. Hold your tongue and let the power of music take over. Let yourself sing from the heart while you sit there in total silence. If you put that one song on repeat and if the song could speak, it would say, "Can you move on already? I'm tired!"

Let every melody, word, and beat release something from your system. Allow the music to lead you to memory lane, then it will help you remember why you were fighting in the first place. Let that song make you stop and reflect on how far you've come and remind you that going back is simply not an option; you can't afford to even entertain such a negative thought. Find a connection within your heart and within your spirit. Then, when you're ready in your own time and in your space, open your mouth and begin to make positive confessions about your situation. Speak on whatever was taking over your mind and, most importantly, proclaim the victory you do not yet see. Once you're done, get up and play some happy music that you like. Don't forget to put a smile on; it suits you. ☺

**"I CAN'T GO BACK TO THE WAY IT USED TO BE, BEFORE YOUR PRESENCE CAME AND CHANGED ME."**

# TEN

### *"Your skills will take you where your bad character will not sustain you."*
**Unknown**

Last week I received a text message from a lady I once worked for in a law firm. It was a temporary contract and she was my manager. She is a lovely lady and working for her was an amazing experience. She told me that she received a call about a job I applied for, asking whether she thought I was a good candidate. The potential employer happened to know her personally, and he wanted some 'off-the-record' information about me. She said really nice things and advised that I should be given the interview and considered for the role. She later called me and told me about the discussion and gave me some interview tips. I was so grateful. If you know any lawyers, one thing they do not have is time, and so her willingness to say great things about me and offer a helping hand truly touched me deeply.

I thought to myself: *Imagine if I had been difficult to work with, rude or even lost it because I was having a bad day? What would she have said when she got that call?* In life, you will never know where your doors will open. You never know who will help you add an additional brick to the building of your future. Over the years, I've had to build my character. I used to be very snappy. I always felt that if someone said something about me, I did not owe them an explanation. I'd give them a response and they were very 'cut-throat', rude responses. The Lord has been teaching me to pick my battles; you don't have to be angry all the time, and you don't have to talk back at all times. Listen more and talk less; even in situations when you know you are right, choose your words thoughtfully. You can never truly change someone's inner perception of you, so instead of spending my life constantly snapping, I choose the high road. I decided to use my time to develop the person that I am so that it does not affect the person I am becoming. In this life, you will work with all types of people, but your inability to control your character and emotions can make you miss opportunities if you are not careful.

I feel as though we have become rude and respect has become the thing of the past, especially within our generation. I say this without biting my tongue (this time). The way that I see certain young people speaking to adults and to their peers is an utter and complete shame. You can no longer tell anyone anything anymore because everyone is now 'entitled' to an opinion, even if that opinion is self-destructive. Dear young people, please know this: The person you choose to become and the bad habits you choose to entertain will never disappear overnight. They will delay your destiny in the real world. NOBODY wants to deal with a person who has major attitude problems. It might seem funny because your friends are clapping for you and cheering you on, but guess what? You are only slowing yourself down.

Do not think that opportunities only come to adults. You can achieve anything you want to achieve right now, but you must start the work on your character and make it a daily task. Some will ask, how can I achieve this? Simple. Choose to change your reaction to the different circumstances that will arise. If you are a person that is snappy, try to be calm about the situation when it comes. If you are a person who swears a lot, try to handle a situation without using foul language. It's not enough to say I am making a change; it is more about putting it into action when faced with issues.

I am not saying change who you are, nor am I suggesting that you allow people to walk over you. What I am saying is change what you do with who you are. I hope you understand. Some people feel like if I was this loud rude person, when shaping my character, I must become quiet. However, this is not true. You can still be loud but choose not to be rude. You can use your loudness to motivate and empower others rather than use it to overpower them.

# WHO YOU ARE VS. WHERE YOU ARE GOING.

# ELEVEN

❧ I ❧

*"There are certain things that are temporarily important, and others are permanently important. The tricky part is learning the difference."*
*Noella Kazadi*

Sometimes, the process of achieving your goals will take slightly longer than you anticipated. It is easy to lose sight of the fact that you exist in a world with people who also need you as much as you need to attain your goals. God might just hold back on certain things for a while so that you can regroup and come back to the 'normal world'. There is more to life than getting that job, the degree or the business opportunity you want. Although I encourage everyone to work extremely hard to achieve their goals, don't lose sight of your surroundings whilst doing it. I worked in a firm recently with partners that pretty much live in the office. They can be at their desks at 7am and leave at 2am, and these people have families, children and partners. I thought to myself, *Well, you are more than excellent at what you do, but surely someone/something must be a sacrificial lamb. In the end, would it all be worth it?*

When I first started my legal career I too was eager to work extremely hard, and everything came second. This had some negative consequences because when I would not get opportunities I knew I worked hard for, I beat myself up about it and felt that my sacrifice was in vain. I would shut down for days and avoid talking to anyone. My view was that hard work should always equal immediate results and if I wasn't getting them, I must have acquired the rights to blame God.

Looking back on that, I now see that it was God's way of slowing me down and giving me time to indulge in the beauty of other things in life. I now understand that although aspirations are important, there will be days when you don't get the results you want, and that's okay. Maybe some of those opportunities will make you lose focus of people or other duties around you that are clearly as important.

Now, with this new knowledge and understanding, what do I do? I still work as hard, sometimes harder than before, but I have more of a balanced life. While I understand that this is my career, I know there is more to life than this. I also understand that some opportunities will not be given to me because God wants to make me stronger. I will be sad about this, yes, because I am human, but I will not be defeated. If I need some time to recharge, I will take the time to do that. Taking time to pause will help me to see ways in which I can improve. Remember that when you die, your degrees, your money, your achievements will not be buried with you. People will remember how you made them feel and how good you were to them, so always keep that in mind. Make time for those who truly matter.

# THE QUESTION IS, ARE YOU TRULY OKAY?

# TWELVE

*"Death and life are in the power of the tongue,
and those who love it will eat its fruit."*
**Proverbs 18:21**

Did you know that you can determine how you start your day? Did you know that you can speak life into your day? Did you know that you can decide to not allow yourself to get angry? I used to have a bad habit of saying, "Today is going to be a bad day," and effectively that day would turn out to be extremely terrible. It is not so much the things that would happen to me during that day, but rather how I would react to those things. It would result in further irritation and an absolute catastrophe!

One of the most important ways to define how your day turns out is determined by the way you start it. I am training myself to not pick up my phone as soon as I wake up, and I know many of you can relate. I used to wake up and I would start to feel with my hand to find my phone even before my eyes were open. I would then spend at least 20 minutes looking through my social media, then I'd say a quick prayer which was literally, "Thank you God, for the breath of life, Amen." I would then jump out of bed and begin complaining about one thing or the other. Most of us do this, but we don't realise how often it happens until we read it from another person's perspective, right?

Whatever I decide to feed my mind with first thing in the morning I know will certainly become embodied within me, and therefore affect my day in a positive or negative way. The changes I've made are not big chunks of changes, but they start to happen gradually and in the long run can create complete transformation. It does not take an expert to wake up tomorrow and choose not to pick up your phone first thing in the morning doing absolutely nothing useful on it. I have now changed my mindset around the manner in which I begin my day, but of course it is still a process.

I believe in the power of prayer. Before I even touch my phone, I take some time to sincerely pray and speak blessings upon my day. I also ask the Lord to grant me the courage and patience to deal with any challenges that may come my way, and most importantly the wisdom to know that I am not defined by those situations. I read a chapter in the Bible because this is my biggest motivator and also gives me great insight into something I am passionate about. I may also decide to read something else that I feel will add to my knowledge and understanding, whether this is a new vocabulary, something historical or even the news. I realised that my phone and social media accounts did not disappear in the process, can you believe that?

My adopted lifestyle changes have left me feeling more positive and driven to face the day. I encourage you to start your day in a positive way. Not necessarily by doing what I do, but by finding a lifestyle that works for you. You might have realised that I am not calling it a routine, and this is because anything that begins to feel like a routine becomes very tedious and boring. So, I choose to make it a lifestyle instead.

Confessing positive things about your day, your life and your surroundings will help you handle those challenging days the world will throw at you. Remember, words have a lot of power. Not just the words we say to others but those we declare to ourselves. What do I advise?

Speak life always.

**A CHANGE CAN BEGIN TODAY IF YOU TRULY WANT IT.**

# THIRTEEN

❦ I ❦

*"They are not your friends until they have defended you in your absence."*
**Unknown**

There will be days where you will not truly see eye to eye with people. I believe this happens for two reasons: To either make your bond stronger, or to separate you from them. It will make your bond stronger once you cross over the hurdle because you will feel a stronger connection or appreciation for them. If you need to separate from them, you will notice that their presence in your life is causing you more pain. I usually narrow it down to intention and understanding.

Something will happen to you and someone near you, and this will show you their intentions in your life. Some people do not intend for you to do well or to succeed. You will find that such people will begin to show negative signs, mainly showing you problems rather than encouragement. It is hard to put exact guidelines, but there will be signs that cause your instincts to speak to you. Regardless of the direction you decide to take, always remember that it is possible for you to be civil with someone without letting them enter your private life.

Secondly, you should understand that there should not be a moment where you can be close to somebody yet have constant lack of communication or understanding that always leads to disputes. The question that I raise is, how understanding is the individual in trying to solve the arising issues? Is it mainly

49

talking to prove a point, or is there actually an effort made in seeking to understand so that a solution can be reached?

Remember life is not always going to be easy, we all need people around us to face the rough days with. However, you are not called to be close to everyone. It is not even advisable to let anyone and everyone in your private life. Some people will come for a while, some people were never meant to be there in the first place and others stay for a long time. Be careful because people may try to disconnect you from the long-term people. You might surround yourself with people who you occasionally fight and disagree with, but you also know they will support and encourage you and, most importantly, have your best interests at heart when it matters the most.

# IT'S NOT ABOUT THE DISAGREEMENT, IT'S ABOUT INTENTION.

# FOURTEEN

*"Success is no accident. It is hard work, perseverance, learning, studying, sacrifice and most of all, love of what you are doing or learning to do."*
*Pele*

I was in France last weekend preaching at a youth conference. All I could think about was how far I have come and how much I did not deserve to be there, but God's grace made it all happen. I thought to myself, *How can this little girl be preaching and motivating old and young people in this strange land?* From the time you hear promises from God about your life, or at the point you set out to achieve goals, to the time you see them coming to pass (such as this book), it will take sleepless nights, sacrifice, hard work, stress and days of wishing you just picked another path. But at the end of it all, you will be living your dreams and feel amazed when it starts to come to pass.

Most people usually set out goals, but very few people experience the accomplishment of these aspirations because they fail to put in the hard work. Just because you're meant to be great does not exempt you from working hard for that greatness. One day you will look back and see how much you have grown due to all the downfalls you faced when you were building your empire. I am now travelling to different countries and cities to preach, and it is not something I can ever get used to. Every day I sit and wonder, *How did this happen?* I am extremely thankful to God for using me to impact lives, and at the same time have my life impacted by the discovered experiences and the people I meet.

You may be a person full of ambition with plans to take over the world. I know many people have told you how impossible your dreams are and how you should be more 'realistic'. Tell them to either sit there and watch you or walk away and look behind their shoulder, because either way you will make it. After that, you make sure that you spend your time working hard, but don't do it to prove them wrong. Do it to fulfil your dreams because trying to prove someone wrong takes energy and focus away from the true intention. Working hard on your dreams will prove them wrong anyway, therefore from where I am standing it is a win-win situation.

# CLIMBING THE INVISIBLE WALL OF SUCCESS.

# FIFTEEN

*"Being a Christian is more than just an instantaneous conversion - it is a daily process whereby you grow to be more and more like Christ."*
**Billy Graham (Rest in Glory)**

If you are a person of strong faith, I am sure that you have encountered people who have questioned your faith. They ask why you believe in God or try to give you 'legitimate' reasons as to why God and Jesus do not and never did exist. Today I want to share my faith journey with you and talk about why it is impossible to separate me from it.

Christianity to me is not a religion. It is not a bunch of rules that I follow to feel better about myself; it is an inseparable part of my life. Some people see this as enslavement or being brainwashed, but it comes down to one thing: My personal encounter with the Creator. It is something that cannot be explained to you. Until you truly have that spiritual encounter, one which cannot be explained by human logic; then, you will understand my faith. It is hard to put us all in one box because everyone has their own personal experiences, which may differ from the next person. But we have one thing in common: We once felt lost until Christ saved us.

I grew up in a Christian family and some say this is the reason these beliefs were 'brainwashed' in my mind. Of course, the mistake that some people make is to believe because of a parent or a family member. The problem is we forget that humans are flawed, and the moment that person acts in a way that we would consider un-Christian, we are quick to leave our faith. I had to arrive to a point where I gained an understanding and accept Christ into my life for my benefit. At that moment, I realised that even when I encounter situations that my parents, my family and my friends cannot necessarily understand, I can always open-up to God.

It is commonly known that God is judgmental and unloving to certain people, but that could not be further from the truth. I know because the God that I had an encounter with is the most unconditionally loving God. Religion will teach you to take specific steps so that you can obtain love from your God. The fundamental aspect of Christianity is for you to come as you are to God and accept that he will transform you, and he loved you even before you acknowledged him. To anyone who has ever felt that they are not good enough to be loved by God, hear this from me: If God can love a person like me, he can love you too, because I am confident that I was undeserving of his love. It does not matter what you have done, as long as you are ready to be changed by him, he will do the rest and you can make that decision today by confessing from your heart with your mouth that Christ died for your sins and you want to start a new walk with him.

The other important aspect of my faith is to live a life of discipleship. I understand that not everyone will agree or relate to me, but that should not stop me from demonstrating the love of God anyway. Most of the time we judge the whole of Christianity because of people's non-biblical ways, but I want you to remember that they are human, and humans have blemishes. This does not redact the fundamental principle of

God being loving. Nevertheless, it is very hard to understand some of these concepts with human knowledge.

When I look at nature and how it functions, I see the evidence of a divine artist. When I observe the way the human body operates, it is almost like a machine, and there is no way this could just happen by mere chance. When I observe the ants and how they gather their foods and build mountains, I am rest assured that above human creation there is a master of the arts, God himself.

I was in my early teens when I had a personal encounter with God. Although I was already in the church, I knew God was 'there', but I had not encountered him. Attending church at the time was a simple routine until I went through a season of hardship. I remember thinking how much I needed to speak to somebody who could understand me. I remember lying face down and crying out to God, and within that moment I felt so much warmth and peace. It was from that moment that I started to grow with him. I felt accountable to him rather than human beings. When I would do wrong I would feel as though I was letting God down, not because I was displeasing my parents, but because God wanted better for me. There is no love or peace like His; I can testify.

I pray that one day you will also encounter the love of Jesus Christ in your life. In the meantime, let us continue to be kind, let us understand that having different opinions in life is not a reason to be hateful. My faith gives me hope in the dark times, prayer gives me strength during the difficult days and Jesus Christ gives me comfort when a hug just does not do it. I cannot make you feel what I feel, but I hope that one day you too can encounter his love in your life.

**THERE WILL COME A TIME IN EVERYONE'S LIFE WHEN LIFE WILL TEACH US THAT WE NEED GOD.**

# SIXTEEN

꩜ I ꩜

*"Individual commitment to a group effort; that is what makes a team work, a company work, a society work, a civilization work."*
**Vince Lombardi**

Have you ever taken the time to observe a relay race? It does not matter how good you are at the race; it is more about the teamwork because you cannot run the whole race alone. It is about understanding everyone's strengths and weaknesses and then figuring out who should run first and last. It is about encouraging one another, even after you run your lap, and respecting everyone's capabilities. Life may put you in various situations where you find yourself in a relay race, but if you only think about yourself and your aptitudes, you will end up losing the race.

You may have the vision to achieve something great, but to achieve it you need to first sit down and be true to yourself. First you must understand that you may be the person with the idea, but you will require help to execute that idea. You will need to acknowledge that there are certain people that are better skilled than you in some areas. Surround yourself with people who understand your vision and share your passion. When you observe a relay, it does not matter who is the last person to receive the baton, they always have a stance of readiness and focus.

It is possible that they don't always see eye to eye, but because they have the same passion, putting differences aside to focus on the prize is easily done. Here are important things to note: Pick your team well, be an effective member of any team and understand everyone's strengths and weaknesses.

# GO ALONE AND GO FAST. GO WITH A TEAM AND GO FAR.

# SEVENTEEN

I

*".....Therefore be wise as serpents and harmless as doves."*
**Matthew 10:16**

EXPERTS!!! There will always be someone who wants to become an expert of your life or situation, whether you realise it or not, whether intentional or otherwise. You have allowed this individual to influence your thoughts and decision-making process. Society refers to experts as individuals or bodies who have studied an area enough for their opinion or judgment to be considered reliable and valuable. For example, when you call a psychiatrist, their job would be to determine whether your actions were conscious driven or not. In a similar manner, we have other self-proclaimed 'experts' who manage to convince you that they care about you, and that no one knows you better than they do.

This is not always a negative connotation; however, you should never allow another person to encourage you to abandon your morals because of the superior position they have decided or that you've allowed them to play in your heart, mind and body. Always ask yourself the obvious question: What is their intention? We have allowed such people to make decisions in our lives or direct our steps because we have lost our self-confidence, and this has happened more than we wish to admit. Then we feel we 'need' these people to give us permission and validation to do things that contribute to our destruction. In the beginning we are unaware that these 'experts' will eventually become negative shapers of our destiny. Do not allow someone to enter your life and ruin it, especially because you do not know whether they will be around forever. These people will not come as devils with horns, that is too obvious. They come disguised as the most understanding, loyal and sympathetic people. Not every person who decides to have an opinion in your life should be given the limelight, neither should you permit what everyone thinks or feels about you to affect you. They are nothing but self-proclaimed experts whose opinions really don't matter. Choose your advisers very wisely.

# WHO MADE YOU THE EXPERT OF MY SITUATION?

# EIGHTEEN

### ❦ I ❦

*"I remember how it made me feel. I remember the smell and the day. I even remember the clothes I wore; I will never forget how his words changed my perspective."*
**Noella Kazadi**

There is a major difference between impact and fame. We can get the two misconstrued by thinking there is a thin line between the two, yet in reality they could not be further apart.

We live in a generation where people are more concerned with being known and being famous. Being identified has somewhat become proof that they have stimulated impact. There are many people in this world that have made a huge impact in our lives and continue to do so, yet, no one knows their names. There are also people who are well-known (famous) but also have great impact in people's lives. Notwithstanding there are also people who are well-known for various (sometimes ridiculous) reasons, but they have not made an impact in people's lives. These people can be entertaining to watch and even to have around, but the question is: What positive impact do they have in our daily lives or future? Maybe not much. Maybe none.

You could aspire to be well-known, which can be deemed as an achievement to some degree, but I will encourage you to positively impact people instead and maybe fame will just naturally come as part of the package. When we speak of impact, many of us think of 'changing the world', standing on big stages, or having some political affiliation. True impact starts with YOU! You cannot positively impact anyone if you have failed to do the same for yourself. Never undermine your small beginnings, never get disheartened by past failures and most importantly, never give up on you. Once you have arrived at a place of 'self-impact', impacting others and situations is an easier task. Many of us seek to become world-changers, but we fail to focus on changing ourselves and our own world.

Another way to make an impact is through the small things that you do each day, because they will end up contributing to the bigger framework. You must start somewhere. You can make a change in one person's life today by simply greeting them with a smile. You will never know the impact it will have on them in that moment, or who they will tell about your act of kindness. And just like that, you are famous too!

# I AM SORRY, I DO NOT RECALL…

# NINETEEN

*"But when her masters saw that their hope
of profit had gone, they seized Paul and Silas
and dragged them into the Market place to the
Authorities."*
**Acts 16:19**

story I was reading in the Bible put so many things into perspective for me. In Acts 16:16-24, the Bible speaks of a slave girl who brought her masters a lot of profit because she was a fortune teller. When I reflected on that scripture, I was left with a few questions. How can the girl have a talent, but remain a slave? Why did her talent bring fortune to others instead of herself? The simple answer to the second question is that her talent was not bringing her income because she was a slave. However, I have thought about it further, and now I understand that she was made a slave because of her talent. Yes, her talent made her a slave.

But how could this be? This leads us back to my first question. I understand that her masters did not like her, nor did they need her, but they needed her talent because it made them profit. This means that in this world, there are people who may be close to you, who may seem to care for you and may even seem as though they are sticking up for you in the same way the masters tried to do later in the verses. However, always ask yourself: Are these efforts made because they care about me or because of their need of me?

When we to apply this biblical event to our daily life, we will find that there are people close to you because you have something that can profit them. As soon as their need of you ends, they will discard you too; do not ever allow yourself to become a slave to somebody else. There are some of you in relationships who go over and above for the person you love (ride or die, they call you), yet your *honey bun* is only present or there when they want something. AGAIN, these people are also skilled at destroying anyone else who dares to get close to you. They know that if anyone else managed to get close to you, you may end up discovering the truth and walk away, so they keep your mind enslaved to think you don't need anyone else. Therefore, I urge you to take a few minutes to read this powerful story and do some self-reflection. The easiest thing to do is bring forward excuses and reasons for a person's behaviour. If a relationship has to develop at the cost of drowning you, alarm bells should start ringing in your mind. Most of the time we know this, but we don't want to accept it. Please be duly advised that knowingly or subconsciously you have become a slave for the benefit of someone else. That is always an unfair deal.

# DO NOT ALLOW SOMEONE TO BE THE MASTER OF YOUR MIND; THINK!

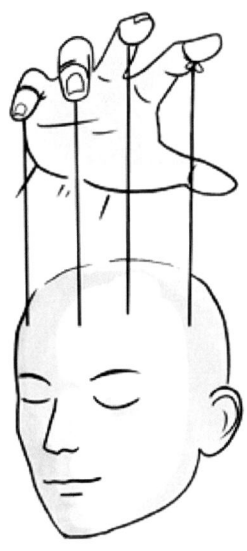

# TWENTY

*"Your success story is more connected to your journey, than your destination."*
**Noella Kazadi**

D o not allow yourself to try and be successful so much that you actually forget to succeed. In earlier chapters, I spoke on the importance of setting goals, having ambition and being focused. So many people say, "If I could go back, I would do this and that differently," even after they have finally obtained their dreams. I believe that it is the journey that makes the destination worthwhile. Therefore, it is right to assert that success is not just the destination but more so the journey to that destination.

Along the journey you will meet different obstacles and blessings. The mistake we often make is that we don't make time to deal with the arising obstacles; we brush them away and continue to chase success. We sadly neither make time to appreciate or give attention to our blessings because we are too focused on getting to the finish line.

Along our journey there are blessings that cross our paths in different ways, some of which we overlook daily. Our families, children and homes are blessings that we sometimes fail to count or make time for. We forget to grab every moment of success because we choose to live a life of regret rather than living in the moment.

In the end, we can end up acquiring the dream job, dream house, dream career, dream husband/wife, but we end up not enjoying or being content because we forgot to enjoy the journey. Remember, time did not stop; it continued alongside you. There are aspects of life that you cannot experience or enjoy retrospectively. It must be lived in the present.

**EVERY STAGE OF YOUR LIFE WILL GIVE YOU A
PIECE TO THE PUZZLE.**

# TWENTY-ONE

*"To see the light of the world is to be the baobab trees, to watch our own leaves seasoned in quarters of a million years only to become gold to the unknown soil, a threat to the sky."*
**Goitsemang Mvula**

My father once told me about the analogy of a baobab tree and the importance of being rooted. He said to me that when you plant a baobab seed, be prepared for a very slow growth. You still need to water this plant a few times a day, in the same way you would for other trees. He told me, you may have a neighbour who plants a mango tree at the exact same time that you planted the baobab tree, but the mango tree will grow faster than the baobab tree.

This can become discouraging for you because you want the results that other people are seeing. Even when you are doing the exact same thing or doing more than them, you are not seeing the same results. After a while, you will notice that the baobab tree has begun to grow (this process can take years), the branches are very strong, and it has the capacity to grow immensely in height in comparison to other trees. This tree is also able to withstand different climates once it is fully developed. My father asked me if I wanted to know why this was so. Of course, I did.

He said that the baobab tree does not show its outer growth instantly because of the work that first takes place in its roots.

In the first few years, the tree develops roots that go very deep into the ground and they equip the tree with the ability to grow extremely high. The roots also give the tree the ability to grab water from the depths of the ground, and this by default grants the tree the power of adaptability in every season. This automatically increases its longevity in comparison to many other trees even though the other trees grew and developed sooner.

There are lessons to learn from the baobab tree; never compare your journey to anyone else's, and don't allow yourself to be discouraged because you are seeing other people succeed. You haven't failed, you just have work to do. You have also perhaps underrated the importance of allowing yourself to be rooted, and this is vital because focusing on your roots first will give you stability in different areas of life. Don't always be quick to see results, because you may not be physically or mentally ready to deal with the speed of the results. Take your time to be shaped and watered; allow yourself to withstand different seasons and situations.

**FIRST, BE ROOTED. YOUR TIME WILL COME.**

# TWENTY-TWO

※ I ※

## *"You cannot recycle wasted time."*
**Noella Kazadi**

One of the causes of time-waste is when you make the deliberate decision to be involved in issues that have nothing to do with you and that you have no control over. There are people who are either inquisitive or trouble makers, and sometimes it is hard to tell the difference. Being either category can result in wasted time, and this can never be recovered. Some people need to understand that they cannot solve everyone's problems or be in between everyone's issues because some things are simply none of your business.

I am not saying you can't be there for someone or be a peace maker, just be mindful that certain situations do not require you to be present. You may desire to make peace between quarrelling parties, but please grow the discernment to know the things which concern you from the ones that simply don't. If you constantly put yourself in the middle of other people's issues, you are wasting the time you could have spent doing something impactful with your own life. Used time does not inevitably equate to time well spent.

Secondly, we also have people in life that are troublemakers, as mentioned above. These types of people will always find time to bring strife and commotion into people's lives. It's a shame because some of them never realise that they will never get back the time they spent doing that. Now imagine that you end up in the same category as people who genuinely mean to do evil, as you have one thing in common: 'wasted time'. Without a question, you need to use wisdom to understand that certain battles are not yours to fight, and certain conversations are not yours to have. Engaging in such is like deliberately making the decision to dig into your pocket and spend your valuable time which, by the way, you will never get back. Get wise and be conscious of where and how you spend your valuable time!

**EVERY DAY YOU GET 1440, PLUS CHOICE OF EXPENDITURE.**

# TWENTY-THREE

## *"A heart at peace gives life to the body, but envy rots the bones."*
### Proverbs 14:30

Envy is a mind game that will make you belittle yourself, your ambitions and your worth. Most of the time we envy what we do not know or understand, and we envy our perception of other people's representation of things or events, which can end up being far from the truth. In this journey called life, you must be careful to not stare too hard because what you see can end up playing on your mind. Everyone has their time and season. Your lack of patience can make you miss your own target because you are busy envying others.

There is nothing wrong with looking up to someone. We all have role models, examples and people we admire. But it is important to understand when it is turning into a setback or, worst case, an obsession. Most of the time we don't understand people's hard work or how long it took them to get to where they are. There's nothing for us to do but to respect other people's hustle and focus on our own.

You should also understand that envy will lead you to believe that what you have is not good enough. You start to wonder why you can't be more like another person or wonder what they have that makes them more special or deserving than you. Once these thoughts invade your mind, they will grow. The more they grow, the more you want to do something about it, no matter what it takes. This can give you an urge to do things for yourself to match up or surpass that person, or worst-case scenario, do something to that person (even if it involves fabricating information, or worst-case, harming the person). My advice is to work hard and earn everything you have in your life. Let your setbacks become your motivation and your persistence mechanism. Repeat after me; social media publications are cherry-picked by the account holder.

**ENVY CAN BOOST YOU TO TAKE SHORTCUTS IN LIFE WITHOUT TRULY KNOWING WHERE THEY LEAD.**

# TWENTY-FOUR

*"So then, because you are lukewarm, and neither cold nor hot, I will vomit you out of My mouth."*
**Revelation 3:16**

I wanted to take a bath today, so I turned on the tap and left the bathroom while the water filled the bathtub. When I returned about 10 minutes later to check on the progress, I touched the water and realised it was only lukewarm. I felt irritated because it wasn't what I wanted; I expected hot water. I tried again and ensured I turned the hot water tap on. I returned after a few minutes and realised that the water was not getting hot as fast as I wanted it to. It made sense for me to pull the plug, let the lukewarm water go down the drain and start again.

Take a second to process what I have just said; I am sure I am not the only person in the world who has done this. In life, nobody has time for lukewarm, 'half-certain and half-committed' people. People who seem to have the potential to go somewhere, yet also have the possibility of going nowhere. It would have been better for me to have cold water instead, because at least I would know what to expect. You need to be a person who is sure of the energy you want to release and be certain of the person you want people to perceive you to be. Nobody wants to be around someone who is unsure about everything.

Another way of looking at it is this: You may need time to empty yourself and restart the process to achieve the best results. Some of us try to add hot water to a lukewarm situation but discover it is actually easier to simply start over. The wisest thing to do is to empty yourself of all the setbacks, ambiguity and half-heartedness, and reset your foundation altogether. Your mind will tell you that you should not empty yourself because you will fall behind, but this is not true. Don't ever be scared to start over if you believe that it is the right thing for you. Remember that no one likes things that are lukewarm, so no one would also want you at your lukewarm stage. Be brave enough to make the decision to restart, even if it means totally changing your circle. This would most certainly be worthwhile.

# THINK, EMPTY AND REFILL.

# TWENTY-FIVE

*"Smile, even though I hurt see I smile*
*I know God is working so I smile*
*Even though I've been here for a while I smile*
*You look so much better when you smile, so*
*smile."*
**Smile – Kirk Franklin**

You are too hard on yourself. Will you just stop for one second? Can you just stop and not think about all the things you need to do, achieve, change, fix and stop? Even for five minutes, give yourself a pat on the back because you are still here, still living and still breathing. You can't be always hard on yourself, you can't always blame yourself for everything or fix it all today. Your worry will not change anything. Think about that one person who needs you. Even if you feel you have no one, as long as you are alive there will be someone who will need you.

I know you haven't heard this lately, or maybe you have but you have not believed it; I appreciate you. I see your hard work even beyond what you show, and I see the purity of your heart. I see you wanting to do and be better. You also need to see this in you, too. No more sleepless nights worrying about yourself or those close to you. Instead we will now choose hope, we will not give up, we will fight. Let us not forget to also laugh, smile, relax, and remember the good days and enjoy the memories.

Don't forget to dream; we will dream of a positive destiny, of more days of laughter, of being there for one another during the tough times and sharing moments of happiness.

We will not stop there because we will remember to wake up from the dreams and choose to live in the moment. Yes, we will bring our dreams to life and live them boldly. We will appreciate the environment, the flowers, the trees, the wind and the blue skies. We will infect others with our positive energy.

When you walk down your street you will smile at the familiar old lady you often see, you will give encouragement to the beggar you constantly bump into, you will say good morning to the familiar faces you see on your daily journeys.

You are doing better than you think, and that is something to be happy about today.

**YOU CAN DO IT! BELIEVE IN YOU.**

# TWENTY-SIX

﹩ I 﨟

*"Don't paint for the eyes, understand the invisible frequency."*
**Noella Kazadi**

I was painting the other day and I realised that the beginning was easy, but after some time, the process just seemed very tedious. Since I had already started, I felt obliged to finish the painting. Eventually I had to move the furniture out of the way so that I could paint behind the hidden walls. For a split second I thought to myself, *Do I really need to paint these parts? Surely, I can get away with simply painting around the furniture, and that will give the impression that the room is totally painted?* Of course, I went on to paint the whole room, but after I sat down and reflected, I understood that in some ways we do that in our daily lives; we consider easier options.

Think about it, how often do you put work into things that other people will see? Even the way you dress? For the ladies it's the perfect make-up and perfect hair, the fashionable dresses and the impressive shoes. For men, you clean up well, you know how to 'talk' your way into a situation, you do certain things to impress your friends; let's not forget the rise of the 'beard gang'. Have you ever stopped and asked yourself: How often do I take time to fix things that have a huge effect on my life, but are not necessarily visible to people's eyes?

Just because you portray a particular image does not automatically mean this is your true identity. Sometimes we put on a front, and to some degree I understand because you cannot show or tell everyone everything about your personal life. Once doors are closed and once no one is looking, how often do you take time to heal? Not for the sake of anyone seeing you, but because you need this for yourself?

Just as I had to move the furniture to paint the hidden walls, have it in mind that one day everything you're covering up with different things will be exposed. When that happens, you will see how deep you've allowed yourself to sink. It may take time, perseverance, self-love, loss, misunderstanding and reflection, but for the sake of you being whole, take the time to invest in your whole self. It's time well spent, and the results will always make the efforts worthwhile.

**EVERY NOW AND AGAIN, YOU HAVE TO PAINT BEYOND SIGHT.**

# TWENTY-SEVEN

☙ I ❧

*"When we fail to set boundaries and hold people accountable, we feel used and mistreated. This is why we sometimes attack who they are, which is far more hurtful than addressing behaviour or a choice."*
**Brené Brown**

Here is a question to think about today: Do you know how to build a wall of boundaries in your life? Do you possess the ability to simply say 'no' and 'yes' when necessary? I find these questions to be of great importance because there will always be people who try to see how far they can push you or see how much they can get out of you. Establishing boundaries with people upholds character more than you can ever imagine. Not everyone should have the privilege to relate with you or know your personal information just by virtue of asking you questions. I would even say that you should not allow everyone to feel so free around you that they could even gain the courage to ask you certain questions. The solution to this is simple: Set boundaries.

I have not lived for long, but within my lifetime, I have learned that the smaller your inner circle is, the more secure you feel. You have more control and less drama. I am a big fan of meeting new people, but I would not immediately place those people within my inner circle until I have taken the time to get to know them. I set boundaries that will protect me, my life and my future. Setting boundaries also means that people cannot just randomly approach you and start discussing other people's business, because you never at any point implied that this is something you entertain. Your boundaries speak for themselves and set the standards on how you expect to be communicated with.

The most important reason for setting boundaries is because most people live in the moment but do not really take the time to think about the future. Let me give you an example. Today you may be in your overdraft, struggling to find a job, barely got your life together, (or you can just be the ordinary person living an ordinary life), but tomorrow you could become a president, a governor or have some sort of influence. Now imagine that you always had your guard down, spoke your life story to any human, animal or tree that would listen. What would happen next? You will find yourself in possible scandals, the subject of rumours that exaggerate details of your life story, because someone will try to take advantage of your position. The best way to avoid this is to set limits with most people and develop a private life that is only shared with a few trusted people, those who are in your inner circle. This is not to say they would never betray you (look at Judas who betrayed Jesus in the Bible), but at least it would give you more control and better judgment to know who it may be. This is much better than you having to suspect your entire neighbourhood.

# ME, YOU AND THE BOUNDARY LINE.

# TWENTY-EIGHT

❦ I ❦

*"The hype will die down, the cheering will stop,*
*the flower petals will cease, can I hold on to this?*
*When life will give me no reason to?"*
**Noella Kazadi**

Many people want to be with you, but how many would actually stay with you? We live in a delusional world that teaches us to act upon impulse, without truly taking the time to fully digest the information or situation we seek to enter. Understand this, anything new always seems better until it gets old. You need to be able to distinguish between the good and the valuable.

Ladies, we don't dispute it; you are young and beautiful. You may have many guys around you that want to date you, be engaged to you and marry you. Nonetheless, ask yourself, how many of these people do I honestly see staying with me for the long run? Think about your bad habits, the parts of your character that are still developing, and ask yourself, do I really see this person sticking around for the journey? You will then realise that although most will want to be with you, a good 99% will not stay with you. What we tend to do is give attention and chances to anyone who asks, simply on the basis that we are attracted to them. We don't take the time to look beyond our initial feelings. We then find ourselves left with heartache, insecurities, pain and other discomforts. For example, if you go to a Pound shop and purchase headphones, they will be well packaged and look good to the eye, but how long would they actually last? I repeat once again, anything new momentarily appears better.

To the gentlemen, we know you take pride in knowing that you can be with any female you desire. However, we all need love and security, and this applies to you too. Think about it, how many of the people who claim to like you or love you would last the test of time? It is very easy to show your good side, but you know your flaws and your struggles. Do you truly think that all the people that give you attention could handle you for a lifetime? Always seek advice from the rightful elders who preceded you in this journey. The simple message I am sending today is that we need to be people who take time to reflect and seek for the right counsel before making major life changing decisions, because this will lead to consequences that affect more than just ourselves.

# THE QUESTION IS, WHO STAYED FOR THE LONG RUN?

# TWENTY-NINE

*"You saw the depth of my heart and you loved me the same, you are amazing God."*
### Indescribable – Chris Tomlin

It is Chapter 24 in my life story, which marks today as my birthday. On significant dates, people normally take time to reflect upon their lives. This can be on their birthday, New Year or when someone close to them passes away. I am sure there are many others, but those are the dominant days for me personally. One thing I'd like to emphasise here is the importance of being authentic in your life. It is so easy to try to conform to the changing norms of society and adapt to politically correct behaviours.

Many of the birthday messages I received today mentioned how people feel my life has positively impacted theirs. I was astounded by the number of people that knew of me, either through my preaching ministry, work and everything in-between, but most importantly I felt the love. I understood that you do not have to be a psychologist to be a good judge of character; many people observe who you are in silence and at the appropriate time make conclusions. Of course, these will not always be positive, but at least you would grow knowing that you have never tried to be anyone else. I live life with the intent to be better than I was yesterday and to never miss the opportunity to fulfil any of my earthly tasks.

I also discovered that it is important to never stop doing good to people, even if you have been hurt by others in your walk. Don't be naïve, but also never live for vengeance. Some people call it karma, but I say vengeance belongs to the Lord. Instead of wasting your time adjusting your character to block, retract, or be cold, spend time to build your character. There are people that still need you now and those who will in the future.

I am excited to discover what the year ahead has in store for me, and I am only slightly worried that I am getting older.

# CHAPTER 24, WARM UP SEASON.

# THIRTY

❧ I ❧

## *"The same pair of lenses can be used to fix or destroy; it all depends on one's vision."*
**Noella Kazadi**

I call this, *The Analogy of the Glasses*. I know not everyone will be able relate to the metaphor, but the explanation will be easy to understand. People who know me will know that I have been wearing glasses for some time now. When I first started wearing them, it was easy for me to remove them and still be able to do daily functions without them. This could be reading, using the computer and using my phone. However, over the years I have realised that the more I have worn my glasses, the ability to carry out tasks without them has been affected. Why is this? A simple answer is that my eyes have now adapted to seeing through the lenses to the extent that my normal vision is blurred without my glasses on.

What shall we liken this to? Some of us have become dependent on people or situations to such an extent that if that person or situation was removed from our lives, we would lose focus (literally). We would lose our vision because our dependency has grown bigger than we care to acknowledge. The only time we become aware of this is when that person is subtracted from the equation. It is good to build networks, to make connections and to construct relationships because this is also a key aspect of human life. However, don't put yourself in a position where you can only see your vision and future through that person's lenses. Some people are transient and once their time is over, you must still be able to function, and most importantly grow, in their absence.

You are the master of your vision. Although you can try and explain it to someone else and they may be able to relate to it, remember, it's your destiny. There are even some lenses you don't have to look through at all because it is not the right fit for you. I am sure you have once tried on the prescription glasses of a friend and found that your good vision became blurry. Once you removed them, it is likely that your eyes suffered from slight discomfort for a few minutes. Why did that happen? Well, it's a no-brainer; you were never supposed to see through those lenses in the first place. The same glasses give the other person better vision but as for you, your vision worsens. Doing this for a long period of time will damage your vision permanently. The better solution is to understand your own vision and follow it.

# I THOUGHT MY VISION WAS BAD...

# THIRTY-ONE

*"And the light shines in the darkness, and the darkness did not comprehend it."*
**John 1:5**

Have you ever been in a dark room for so long that your eyes begin to adapt, and you begin to slightly see? You must always judge these situations in two aspects and examine which one you fit into. You can be going through a dark moment right now and it feels as if there is no way out. You feel stuck, you feel stranded and alone, and you might feel misunderstood. Please remember that even in the midst of your darkness, there is still hope. You must keep on fighting and keep on believing that the little light you see, even after you have been in the darkness for so long, can be motivation for you. You can stand up and go and look for a bigger and brighter light instead of staying down.

The second aspect is that at times, you have found yourself in a dark place for so long that the little glimpse of light has made you dwell there longer, because although you are able to see a little in that darkness, you have now made the choice to continue to stay there. It has become comfortable for you to stay in the darkness because this is what you have come to know and understand. If this is where you are, you need to gain the strength to get out of that darkness because you won't see the significance of someone coming in and turning on the light for you. You won't see it as a saving grace. Instead, you will cover your face to give yourself the illusion that you are still in darkness because you can no longer handle the strength of unrestricted light.

What is the consequence of the former in comparison to the latter? With the first situation, you will use your darkness as a testimony to others because you were able to survive by using the little light you have. You will work your hardest to ensure that you never get back to a dark place again. With the latter, you will realise that no matter how many lifelines you get, you will always find yourself back in the place of obscurity because you have conditioned your mind to adapt to darkness. This will make you miss bigger and better opportunities that may be found on the other side, because you refuse to challenge the situation. It is time to get up and walk out of darkness.

**AT FIRST, IT'S BLACK, AND THEN IT'S GREY. EITHER WAY, THE CHOICE IS STILL YOURS.**

# THIRTY-TWO

*"...For man looks at the outward appearance, but the Lord looks at the heart."*
**1 Samuel 16:7**

Someone recently said to me, "You always have smiley pictures on your profile; you must be a very happy person." I chuckled inside, because that was far from the truth. As I reflected on this, I noticed it's in the same way someone can ask you, 'How are you?' You are just doing it to be polite and appear nice; you don't really want to sit there and hear how they are or listen to all their problems. You then wait for the 'I am fine' response and repeat the same question another day. In this generation, we have become very selective human beings who give the impression that we have our lives together.

With the growth of social media filters and endless selfies, we are beginning to lack a real human experience. I told the person, "I am not really a very happy person all the time, I simply choose to post happy pictures. On some of the days that I take smiley pictures, I am actually annoyed, but I smile for the camera then return to my annoyance." Do you realise how ridiculous that sounds? I mean, did anyone force you? Yet, most of us have been guilty of this.

Imagine what could happen if we spent less time on being selective about what version of ourselves we show to the world. What if we didn't focus on showing that we're happy when we're not, or if we stopped putting out a lifestyle that we truly don't have? What would happen if we spent that time on developing ourselves, building our self-esteem, learning to love ourselves regardless of people's judgements instead? Imagine we asked questions we want answers to and were ready to listen when people opened up. We would be a step closer to becoming better human beings.

# IS THERE A FILTER FOR A BROKEN HEART?

# THIRTY-THREE

*"The most dangerous thing in life is to not try
based on another's failure."*
**Noella Kazadi**

I lost my earphones, so I asked my sister to lend me hers. She agreed, but she mentioned that only one earphone worked. I was so desperate for earphones that day I took them regardless. I remember that night, putting one earphone in my ear and accepting the difficult experience of speaking on the phone. The following day, I decided to listen to music and once again I put in one earphone. Having the sound only coming out of one ear was irritating, so I decided to try the other one and to my biggest surprise, it worked! The first thing I thought was my sister lied to me, but upon careful consideration, I realised that I did not even try putting both in. My initial experience was a direct result of trusting someone else's experience.

I thought of the many times we miss opportunities because we didn't attempt something based on someone else's failed experience. Perhaps the earphones were not compatible with her devices, perhaps there was something wrong with her phone and not the earphones, perhaps they had even seized working that time. I guess we'll never know. However, what is certain is that if I did not try the other earphone, I would have spent the whole day listening to music from one ear out of ignorance.

My point is that each person has their own experience, but do not stop yourself from chasing your dream, from applying for a certain job or from knocking on certain doors based on certain failure statistics. Why can't you be the exception to the rule? Better, why can't you be the first person to break-through? If you live your life dictated by other people's experiences, you will never get anywhere.

I remember when I decided to become a lawyer. I used to work part-time as a support-worker while I was studying. I remember telling everyone that I was going to study law. I knew that it was the only thing I wanted to do, but people told me, "Don't you know that black people don't get anywhere with law? You will never find a job." Some even told me about people they had known who had studied law, and after spending years looking for jobs with no positive outcome, decided to change career paths. I was advised that the best thing for me to do, as a black person in England, was nursing, because at least I had the security of obtaining a job.

I remember telling them that I did not come on this Earth to simply incur security. I came to be great and I will not be taking shortcuts. I had no problem with nursing, except it was just not what I wanted to do. I found it absurd and unthinkable for me to let go of my dreams for a wage slip. I was more prepared to die trying, to be honest.

A few years later, I was in a skyscraper in one of the top law firms in England. I looked out the window and everything looked so tiny from up there. I closed my eyes and asked myself, *Noella, what on earth are you doing in this building? How did you even get here?* I thought of all the discouragement and the hardship, and I knew in my heart it was very much worth the pain. The sleepless nights, the many rejected job applications, the lost friendships, the opposition and the sacrifice. It had all been worth it.

My brother went out with me in Birmingham once. I remember we had printed out a lot of my CVs and we went around giving them to different law firms. (I do love you, bro!) I remember something that he said to me, it will stay with me forever. He said, "Look, we will go and give CVs to every law firm, because the worst they can say is NO." I guarantee you, not even one of those places called me back, but that day I gained something else; I developed 'tough skin'. Now, I can knock on every door and I will speak to anyone. I will try my best to make sure I reach my destiny because since that day, someone saying no to me no longer knocks me down. It gives me more adrenaline to try again.

After reading this, I hope you gain the courage to chase after your dreams. I do not speak to you as a finished product, I speak to you as a young person who continues to chase after her dreams, as a person who will not give up on her dreams. I am a person who does not allow another person's experience to overshadow my opportunities. I am driven by my vision, I refuse to be knocked down by statistics. Keep pushing, keep believing, keep hoping and I promise you, everything you aspire to do is absolutely doable. I am not deviating your mind from the hardship which will accompany this journey because you will have days where you wished you just listened to them and picked a secure option. Those days exist. But remember, life is far beyond today's wage slip.

# CAN YOU FORGIVE YOURSELF FOR ALLOWING SOMEONE'S FAILED EXPERIENCE TO INFLUENCE YOUR DECISION?

# THIRTY-FOUR

❧ I ❧

**"What a caterpillar calls the end of the world, the master
calls a butterfly."
Richard Bach**

You are not the same person you were when you first started, did you know that? When people decide to leave you because they claim that you have changed, if you believe you changed for the better, do not worry. Unfortunately, not everyone will understand the change, and this is the butterfly effect. You are certainly not the same person you were before because you are more resilient. You are less of a walk-over, you are no longer gullible because you have learned from your past mistakes. You have found yourself, you have grown and evolved. You have outgrown some friendships, seasons and situations, and that is okay.

One of the worst things you can do is become stagnant; having the same friends, being part of the same environment, putting yourself in the same hurtful situations and refusing to move forward. You will need to take a moment to reflect and feel proud of your journey. Some people will try to hold you back because they no longer relate to the new and improved you. The biggest mistake you could make is to allow these stagnant situations to dilute your greatness.

A caterpillar changes into a butterfly and endures the period of transformation. Once that transformation is complete, the butterfly flies away and is never a caterpillar again. I have never seen a caterpillar and a butterfly spending time together or having a catch-up. When I ask myself why, I understand that a caterpillar does not fly. The butterfly flies, but for them to be mates, one of them would have to make a sacrifice. In this situation, only the butterfly can do that, but to accommodate the caterpillar, would be giving up its ability to be free. It would be sacrificing its ability to fly high and view the world from an elevated perspective.

You should not apologise for being able to see the world from a different perspective, nor do you need to back pedal. A butterfly knows what it's like to be a caterpillar, but the caterpillar does not know what it's like to be a butterfly. It will either acquire understanding through experience of evolution, or merely die a caterpillar. Ask yourself: Is it ever worth compromising your growth because of another person's inability to understand or support your new journey of peace and success?

# WOW, YOU HAVE CHANGED! YES, I HAVE. IT IS THE BUTTERFLY EFFECT.

# THIRTY-FIVE

*"Do not desire superficial change you did not work hard for. Rather, dedicate yourself enough to see consistent outcomes."*
**Noella Kazadi**

I have come to the realisation that for you to fully have the best outcome, everything in life needs to follow a strategy. My father recently resumed going to the gym and he became slightly obsessed. He was going every day for the first few weeks. He said you could go to the gym for one hour every day, but that hour will be void if the other 23 hours are not used properly. You need to choose to live a healthy life-style, which means you need to cut out unhealthy eating habits, drink plenty of water and accompany this with a positive mindset.

Health is not simply limited to the one-hour gym sessions twice a week; you need to make a mental decision to make it your lifestyle in order for you to see the full results of your commitment. The same applies when someone decides to go on a diet; that person becomes motivated and they change their eating habits. They exercise 3 times a day and within the following months they see mind-blowing results. This goes wrong when they become too comfortable with the new and improved body and decide to slow down, thus, reverting to bad eating habits. Before you know it, you are now bigger than you were before you decided to go on a diet. You need to realise that to get the best results, you must follow a structured plan.

I am in no way attempting to give you dietary lessons; I am rather showing you that this same theory can be applied to many areas of our lives. Sometimes we don't put the required importance on the background work, and we focus too much on the actual or immediate task. Other times we focus so much on going out with our friends, our partners or a family member that we become content in knowing you made yourself available. The most important thing is not always the physical time spent, but rather the care given when the spotlight is not on you. There are some people who are very good friends, yet they do not see each other often. They know their friend cares for them and the time they do get to see each other. They simply rekindle the pre-existing care and friendship.

This is the same way I also view Christianity. Being a Christian isn't just about the Sundays we spend in church. True Christianity is demonstrated through the moments that we are not at church. This can be the way you treat people, the way you talk and the way you choose to conduct your life. I am a firm believer that Christianity should not always be shouted from your lungs, but instead be shown through behaviour, letting your actions arouse curiosity in people. This will lead them to notice that there is something different about you, and that is always a good place to begin a conversation.

**AFTER THAT ONE HOUR OF WORKING OUT, I DESERVE A WEEK OF TREATS.**

# THIRTY-SIX

*"You are called to be excellent at what you were born to do. That could be one or several things."*
**Noella Kazadi**

When I was younger I loved reading. I did not really have a preferred genre, I would read anything from an autobiography to a high school romance. Reading constantly helped me improve my reading skills and gave me knowledge about various topics. I used to write a lot too, I was one of those kids who confided in 'dear diary'. In hindsight, I can say it was my coping mechanism because I never spoke about my feelings; I wrote them down instead. In one of my daily reflections, I thought it would be a great idea for me to be a writer because I was very passionate about it, and I found it quite enjoyable. Around the age of 10, I remember thinking, *Well, this is great. I have finally found my purpose.*

But life took a slight U-turn when I started high school. I still read books and still wrote, but I discovered that I wanted to be a lawyer. I was not in any of the top sets in my English class, but I was very good at debating and getting my point across. One of the hardest decisions in my life was deciding what I wanted to be. I decided that law was definitely my career path. I read less and less as the years went by, and I admit that the rise of technology did not help. At some point I even stopped writing. I stopped reading because I realised that it was not for me because I could only excel in one thing. I even went as far as destroying all my diaries. Nevertheless, my passion never left; it remained in a clouded state at the very back of my mind.

I began preaching when I was 14 years old and I started going on TV when I was 16 years old. I would be in school from Monday to Friday, and then go to church after school. On weekends, I would be in London, returning to Wolverhampton in the early hours of Sunday morning. On Sundays, I would be standing up for most of the church service as part of my duties. One day I looked back at this and I realised that I could be anything I wanted, and most importantly, as many things as I wanted to be. I do not have to kill my other dreams and aspirations and focus only on one.

You do not need to feel guilty for having more than one passion. From a very young age, God always prepared me to do many things at the same time. We sometimes joke with the people from my church that we have been tired since 'Challenge Me' (inside joke). I am not saying go and be a pilot, an astronaut, a surgeon, an athlete and a lawyer all at once (unless you feel you can, by all means go for it). What I am saying is that some people only want one thing in life and they focus on that one thing for the rest of their lives. However, if you are like me, you have one main goal and other aspirations that you want to fulfil, and this is okay. I mean, if this was not the case, then maybe someone should tell Richard Branson to stop making everything Virgin.

Once I got over my fears, I took out my laptop and I started writing again. I came up with a concept for a book and decided to write, and you are reading it right now.

I encourage you to also face your fears, organise your time, set your priorities and fulfil your dreams. The failure of one dream should never obliterate all the dreams you have. Smart people will learn from their errors in the same way emotional people will decide to quit. Be the smart one. As my mother would often say, "The people who accomplish great things in this world don't have two heads." (Try saying that sentence out loud with an African accent, it's funnier). Do not tell yourself you are not ready; your whole life has been preparing you for such a moment and it is never too soon to start planning your next step. So, what are you waiting for?

Stop reading this book right now! Go and make your plans, but come back to it later, of course. The title is not 36 days of reflection, don't start slacking now.

**I WAS DREAMING THAT I WOKE UP, BUT I WAS STILL ASLEEP. HAVING ANOTHER DREAM.**

# THIRTY-SEVEN

☘ I ☘

## *"Despite your gift, remember that professionals are formed, and not born."*
**Noella Kazadi**

I was at a concert and I was incredibly impressed as I watched the skill of the guitarist. He did not even have to look at his guitar once, he just danced and smiled as he played. It seemed effortless for him, as easy as it is for me to walk. I was in awe, staring at him for ten minutes before allowing my mind to sink into my imagination. I saw him looking at a guitar like it was a weirdly shaped toy as his parents took him to his very first guitar lesson. I saw him at his first school talent show, with his head down the whole time as he tried his latest set. He played two notes and his family stood up and clapped with joy. I imagined him being 12 years old, and he does not play guitar anymore because he is not improving fast enough. He decided that music was not for him. His parents think of all the money they spent for his music lessons and they became annoyed at the teachers because it is easier to be angry at the grown-ups.

Then he turned on his TV one day and saw a professional guitarist, and thought, *Wow! I want to be just like him one day, I want to perform on world stadiums. I could be very good at it if I just practice more.* He commits to playing his guitar again, his head is always down when transitioning from one chord to another. The only time he brings his head up is when he is reading the musical notes in front of him, because he has not yet mastered the ability to memorise all the chords.

I imagine him in his early twenties. His confidence has developed, and he is now the best musician in his neighbourhood. He plays for bands and local acts in small gigs, and he is admired by his friends and fans. His parents are very proud of him and they never fail to remind him. He feels that he is ready to take the next step and applies for a national audition for a chance to be a worldwide musician. He wants to play with bigger bands, to accompany bigger singers. He arrives at the audition with confidence, but as he hears other guitarists playing, he realises that he is not as good as them. His name is called out, but he doesn't hear it. He drifts towards the doubts of his own mind, until he feels a touch on his shoulder. He returns to reality, where a tall, impatient and intimidating man tells him, "We are ready for you." He decides to try anyway, and he plays his piece, but the outcome is devastating. They tell him to find another career because he is not good enough. I imagine him being crushed, disheartened and upset.

He stops playing the guitar, he becomes angry at the world, including himself. He can no longer bear to look at his guitar. Then one day his mother buys him a new one, showing him an old photo of him at his very first talent show, telling him how he could barely remember the two chords. He laughs with embarrassment, now knowing what he must do. And so, he practiced. He had many more failed auditions that only led him to practice more. Then one day, someone believed in him enough to give him a chance.

The outcome? His schedule is now ridiculous. He has a two-year waiting list of people who have booked him to perform on tour with well-known and famous bands.

I clicked out of my imagination and watched him play the guitar. His passion for music was evident in his performance. He excited the crowd, he naturally attracted attention and poured energy into the guitar. It was undeniably remarkable to be in that room, witnessing his dream come to life. I realised if you practice anything continuously, you will eventually become good at it. If you aren't convinced, just ask your parents or elders about the day you took your first step.

Keep practicing, keep believing and soon you will also be a professional in your field.

**GET UP, TRY AGAIN.**

# THIRTY-EIGHT

*"The lack of forgiveness can be likened to you drinking poison but expecting the person who hurt you to die."*
**Bishop T D Jakes**

Y̶ou must let it go now; it's costing you more than you think. We have heard people speak on the importance of forgiveness, and because we want our heavenly Father to forgive us, we must learn to forgive others too. Many people don't take the time to consider the effects of not forgiving. I do not need scientific or spiritual evidence to prove that the lack of forgiveness is toxic. All I need to do is speak to somebody who has taken the decision to not forgive and ask them about the destruction that decision has caused. Today I was thinking about my own life and realised I was that person. I was angry because I held grudges, and this left me feeling entitled to be angry with people for eternity. When you don't forgive, you complicate your life by dwelling on the pain that a situation or person caused you, and then build your life around holding onto that experience, and this will only have a ripple effect.

The sad thing is that you experience the hurt every time you think about it. Picture yourself falling and hurting yourself. You are bleeding and you are in excruciating pain, but after a few days, the wound starts to dry off and the bleeding stops. You decide to peel off the scab, and of course, the wound begins to bleed again, and the pain returns. If you were to take a knife and stab that wound, can you picture the pain?

Sometimes we don't forgive because we feel it minimizes the severity of what was done to us, but that is not the case. Forgiveness is more self-focused, because it is a way to set yourself free from the prison of that person or situation. It doesn't mean that you will be okay and fully recover from the trauma on the same day, but you must be determined to grow away from that period so that you can move towards a better future. When I discovered this, I began my process of change because I realised that I still held grudges towards people who had since moved on. Some had probably made their peace with God and I had chosen to suffer for something I did not do. It just wasn't worth it. The lack of forgiveness and holding a grudge takes a lot of effort; being angry at a situation that has passed is a waste of my precious time in this life.

How would you know that you have truly reached a place of forgiveness?

I would say it is when you see the person, think or remember the negative experience or situation and it doesn't bother you or affect your day. You need to have an even greater understanding to not even think of the situation every time you see them, simply because you have moved on. Some of you might remain friends and build back the bridges that were burned down, while others understand that one can control their change but not others'. Either outcome is still okay, forgiveness is a different process for us all. I think it is better to let go off past pain because it's not worth your peace.

You have a bright future ahead, don't delay your journey any further. The lack of forgiveness is not a sign of strength; it is a sign of weakness and hurt. You are stronger than you think. Choose happiness.

## THE WOUND CAN'T HEAL IF YOU KEEP PEELING IT. IT'S TIME TO LET IT GO.

# THIRTY-NINE

*"Tough days, hard decisions and hopeless*
*moments; are also part of life's package."*
**Noella Kazadi**

My spirit felt anxious when I woke up this morning. I wasn't even sure if I should share this day with you. Part of me has embraced the run of positive days thus far, but I worry that the mention of this day would create inconsistency. I've thought about it carefully and I have decided to share it with you because it will help someone someday.

I found it difficult to pray this morning. I have been unwell for the past two days and I believe my body and spirit is just overwhelmed by life.

I left my job a few months ago because I felt that the role was not for me. I spoke to my dad about it because I needed some advice. He encouraged me to weigh up my options, to think it through before I made a permanent decision. He also insisted that I should do what I feel is best for me. Most people advised me against it, because to them it was more logical to find another job first. Unfortunately, there are times in your life when you just know that your time is up, and that was my time. So, I left without securing another role. I stopped living my life by societal norms a while ago, and I don't advocate torturing yourself by staying in a place that you feel is not benefitting you. The money will not justify it. I figured this is the time to do it, while I am still unmarried and don't have anyone depending on me. I know that once you have more responsibilities, decisions like these become harder.

After about three weeks of being out of work, I was offered a job by an old firm I used to work for. Even though it wasn't a progressive role, I felt that the opportunity was fantastic. I was due to start the role immediately, and I did not need to attend an interview because the manager was already aware of my capabilities. That night I dreamt that it was Monday and I was heading to the job, but someone was telling me that the job was not for me. They said, "You cannot be going backwards, you must come and work for us, because there is a chance of progression." When I woke up, I felt that the dream wasn't random at all, it had a message. I prayed over it and I felt a strong conviction that although the new job was a very good role with a good company, it was just not for me. I battled with myself for a few days, trying to convince myself that it was just a dream, but my instincts were strong.

I turned down the job. I had a feeling that I would get a call from a mystery person, offering me my 'dream job'. It felt like it would happen in a few days, but weeks went by without news. I applied for many roles. Not even one person got back to me. I thought to myself, *I should have taken that job,* because the silence created room for doubts. Deep down I knew that the job was not for me.

After about three weeks of nothing, I received an email from a firm stating that they would like to interview me for a role that had an opportunity of progression. I was very excited! I went for the interview and I performed at my best. A few days later, I received a message confirming that I had made it to the second round of interviews. My confidence grew back instantly. Imagine in the interim, I was offered another interview for a temporary role, but I declined it because I was looking for something more permanent. I truly believed that I would get this job anyway.

I attended the second interview and although it went okay, I wasn't entirely happy with the salary they were offering. I did not dispute it because I knew I would receive training for the role, and this would help me progress. To me, right now, the opportunity to thrive and develop is more important than the money. I did not apply for any other jobs because I was certain this was the job for me. So, when I woke up today, I realised that it has been 9 days since I went for the interview, but I still have not heard back, and this is usually a bad sign.

As I mentioned above, I could not pray, but I managed to mumble a quick prayer. I developed the courage to email the firm, and within 5 minutes I got a response. I was right; I did NOT get the job. In that moment, I thought of all the job opportunities I declined and started to feel like I'd made a mistake. I pulled myself together, prayed, thanked God, read my bible and applied for more jobs.

As the day went on, Abraham was upon my spirit. He knew God had spoken to him about giving him a son. However, waiting on God's time made him become doubtful at some point, so much that he even went outside God's plan and took Sarah's servant. God put this upon my heart; just because it does not happen the way you expected it to, does not mean you've made the wrong decision. You must keep believing.

As I speak to you, I am jobless, but I still believe that there is something better for me. I am certain it will happen before I finish this book. Today I learned that cost comes even with the right path. Hang in there, you are not crazy; it will make sense in the end.

**EVEN THE RIGHT PATH COMES WITH A COST OF ITS OWN. DON'T SECOND GUESS YOURSELF. IT WILL HAPPEN.**

# FORTY

*"Settling down should never turn into a race or competition. Better yourself, make an informed decision and always trust God."*
**Noella Kazadi**

Dear Husband, this is for you.

There are few things you need to know and understand. I am now 24 years old and, according to most people, you should have married me by now. We should have at least one child, apparently. Considering society's expectations, you are running way behind schedule. I am sure many young women of my age can relate to this. Some people get married to an incompatible partner because of the external pressure, others are fortunate enough to marry 'The One' and live happily ever after.

If you are reading this, please understand that there is no rush. I know I have a whole lifetime ahead with you. I know that God is the best planner and luckily for you I do not give in to pressure, and neither should you.

Relationships are a very touchy topic; there are far too many of you rushing to keep up with time. You feel like you ought to be married by now because your friends, your younger sister and your Facebook friends are married. That alone should be a sign to show you that perhaps you have more to learn.

Marriage is a personal commitment. Ladies, sometimes we focus too much on the wedding, the dress and the playlist. I am not against this; however, just remember that once all guests head home, you now have to face your marriage. I have seen people get married and then get divorced less than a year later. I have seen people get married a little older than expected and they are happily married for a long time. I am not saying you shouldn't aspire to be married young, or that you should not seek happiness. I am simply saying that it's okay to take your time and everyone's journey is unique.

I have observed plenty of marriages in my lifetime, both good and bad. My conclusion is this: Deciding to get married should not be as simple as deciding whether to wear heels or flats. Consider all factors, seek good advice, take all the time you feel you need, and enjoy the moments you have alone, because this season is a blessing too.

I have spoken to young ladies who may also feel like they have found The One. I tell them that it's okay to seek more guidance and knowledge, it's okay to spend more time getting to know the person you plan to spend the rest of your life with. Remember that God is love and this should always be the standard. If your beloved truly loves you, make sure he is reflecting godly attributes within his character. Make sure you are also a reflection of the expectations you have for him.

I have spoken to men, too. Please do not assume that being a man automatically gives you access to all the good women. Take your time to seek God and treat your beloved with the respect you would want your sister, mother and daughter to be shown. Treat her the way Jesus would treat the church, remembering the sacrifices he made. Don't forget, even when the church did not understand him, Jesus still loved and protected that same church.

It is okay to seek advice from the people who have travelled this journey before you. Some people say it is not about getting married, it is about *staying* married. I think it is beyond staying married; it should be about staying happily married, even though it will not be sunshine every day.

Dear husband, I know you understand.

# THIS IS NOT A LOVE STORY, THIS IS A TALE OF DESTINY, FOLLOW YOUR PATH.

# FORTY-ONE

*"A daughter needs a dad to be a standard against which she will judge all men."*
**Unknown**

It was Father's Day in England and my father was not with us because he travelled to Congo. It was an odd feeling because we normally rush to him and show him how much we appreciate him. I sent him a text message letting him know how much I appreciate him and thanked him for everything he has done in my life. In less than five minutes he responded, and that brought so much comfort to my heart.

I thought of people in similar circumstances, where they were also not able to be with their fathers. I thought of those who can't even send a text message to their father because he has passed away. I decided to count my blessings. I am blessed.

Sometimes we take people we love for granted, and we don't appreciate their presence in our lives. Life is short. Make time to appreciate and love your family, tell them everything that is in your heart.

Young people, don't be busy pleasing your friends, yet forget to spend time with your parents. While you need their encouragement and approval, they also need your support and attention.

Established adults, I know you may not live with your parents anymore because you now have your own children and families. I do understand, but please remember to check on your parents. One day you will be old, and you would want sincere contact from your children, wouldn't you? Make it less about ticking off a task on your to-do list and more about showing genuine interest in your loved ones.

My father, Dr Claude Lubobo Kazadi, is a rare and wonderful human being. I don't think that this book has enough words for me to explain to the readers just how incredible he is.

But I'll try.

To my father: One day I was speaking to your sister and she told me that even when you were younger, you would always say that you would go to Europe one day. She said you were a determined and driven person from a very young age. The thing I love the most about you is your ability to always use your platform to motivate and uplift others. You know when to stand and defend your beliefs, but most astoundingly you also know how to hold your peace and not convince people of who you already know you are. Many people cannot achieve in two lifetimes what you have already achieved in one. I have had the grace to meet the many people you grew up with and also to meet people that watched you grow. They share a similar testimony about you, they say you have helped each of them in some way.

You are not the type of person who can be bought by material things or earthly positions, and there have been countless times when you have stood firm to what you believed, against every wind and storm. If there are still people in this world who are yet to meet you, surely, they have heard mention of your name by now. If not, the impact you have had on another life will ensure they know your name soon enough.

The world needs to hear your story, it is the tale of a living legend. From the bottom of my heart, thank you Papa.

# WE WILL FOLLOW YOUR FOOTPRINTS TO GREATNESS.

# FORTY-TWO

**"I learned that courage was not the absence of fear, but the triumph over it. The brave man is not he who does not feel afraid, but he who conquers that fear."**
**Nelson Mandela**

Is it not strange that sometimes you find yourself being afraid of something you haven't experienced? You are so scared, you feel sick just thinking about it? I am sure we've all been told about the impact of fear.

Someone once told me that fear can be abbreviated as: 'False Emotions Appearing Real'. I thought about it and saw how I could relate. I thought of the times I have been too scared to take action or to venture down unknown paths. After I developed the courage to do it despite my fear, I realise that it wasn't as bad as it seemed, so I guess the doubts were just in my head. On some occasions I blamed other people, convinced their discouragement had caused my fear. I decided that they were responsible for installing fear into me.

Now I understand that while I am not in control of what people decide to tell me, I am in control of how I let this affect me. Someone can trigger your fear, but if you develop the willpower to fight it, fear will no longer have the capacity to swallow your destiny.

Do you remember fearing the dark as a child? You'd find it hard to go to sleep because you worried about monsters coming to get you. In your mind, monsters dwelled in the dark and so you understood the dark to be unsafe. Maybe you grew up and laughed at the fact that your heart would skip beats for such a trivial thing. Now picture a situation that is making you scared in the same manner. It is not as deep as you think, is it? You've programmed your mind to believe there is reason to hold onto fear, but you must change your mindset.

When we think of great leaders, such as Barack Obama or Nelson Mandela, we consider them as superhumans because of their bravery and determination. However, in reality they have blood flowing through their bodies just like you and me. I am certain they have probably lived through days that left them afraid of the journey they embarked upon, but what would have happened if they allowed their future to be determined by that fear?

You have greatness inside you, but you must now put it in the spotlight. Is the fear you hold worth giving up your destiny? Use it as adrenaline, conquer the impossible and refuse to settle for less than you deserve. The problem is not the person who fails a thousand times and tries again, but rather the person who had a thousand tries and did not try once. Being fearless does not mean that you will not encounter obstacles, rejection or hardship, or that you won't feel fear; it means that despite the hardship, you will find a reason to keep going.

Do not stop now, don't give up! One day you will laugh about your fears as easily as you laughed about being scared of the dark. (I hope you are still not scared of the dark)

**I FEAR FAILING, BUT THIS IS DUE TO MY LACK OF TRYING TRIGGERED BY MY FEARS.**

# FORTY-THREE

※ I ※

## "Addiction is the only prison where the locks are on the inside."
**Unknown**

ddiction: Dependency, craving, habit, enslavement, compulsion and fixation. These are just some synonyms of what addiction is. This is a sensitive subject to talk about, isn't it? We would rather live in denial and make excuses than admit that we have an addiction. We certainly don't want to talk about it.

I believe that everyone has some sort of addiction that they are fighting to overcome or have fought at some point in time. Yet only a few people are willing to admit this. As humans, we consider ourselves experts at diagnosing other people's addictions. We can be judgemental and lack understanding. We say, "If she knows it is bad for her, why does she continue doing it? Why won't she just stop?"

It is too easy and cowardly to judge another person because of their addiction. We may not share that same weakness, but we demand people to sympathize with us about our weaknesses. This is the highest level of hypocrisy. We should still speak up when someone has developed a habit that is destroying them, but we must remember to always come from a place of love and offer constructive advice. It should be because you want that person to seek help, rather than pushing them deeper into isolation and banish them to a dark hole of loneliness.

We are all fighting different issues, and we all have weaknesses that we want to overcome. Let's learn to help each other as though we were helping ourselves. If somebody decides to open up to you, you have a duty to protect them and help them, or at least direct them to someone who can. Fighting an addiction can feel like a lonely experience with no way out.

It helps to come to a point where you can admit to yourself that you have a problem. That's the first step in finding a solution. You have probably indulged in your addiction for so long because you have convinced yourself that there is a good reason for it. You hold onto the 'good' reason instead of acknowledging the fact that the continued commitment to your addiction will eventually destroy you. This means that you have lost the willpower and self-control to want to change. Please, do not die in silence; speak up.

A wise man once told me that a spoken problem is a problem half-solved. I agree with that because speaking to the right person can truly help you unload heavy burdens. It is then that you can begin the process of change.

Just remember that the word 'addiction' in the dictionary does not have your face next to it. This means that other people have gone through what you are going through, and you are not the first and only one. God loves you regardless of your flaws and he is still willing and ready to help you through the journey of rehabilitation. Accept what may seem to be temporary shame or weakness, because you have spoken about it. I have faith that eventually you will be glad that you did.

Addiction does not respect age, gender, culture or background, so be careful what you expose yourself to; be wise. We are not made of brick; we have blood flowing through our veins. There are things that you may swear never to get involved with, but if you expose yourself to it long enough, you will lose track of how you got in so deep. Your life matters. You still matter. Get help.

# "JUST THIS LAST TIME," SAID THE ADDICT.

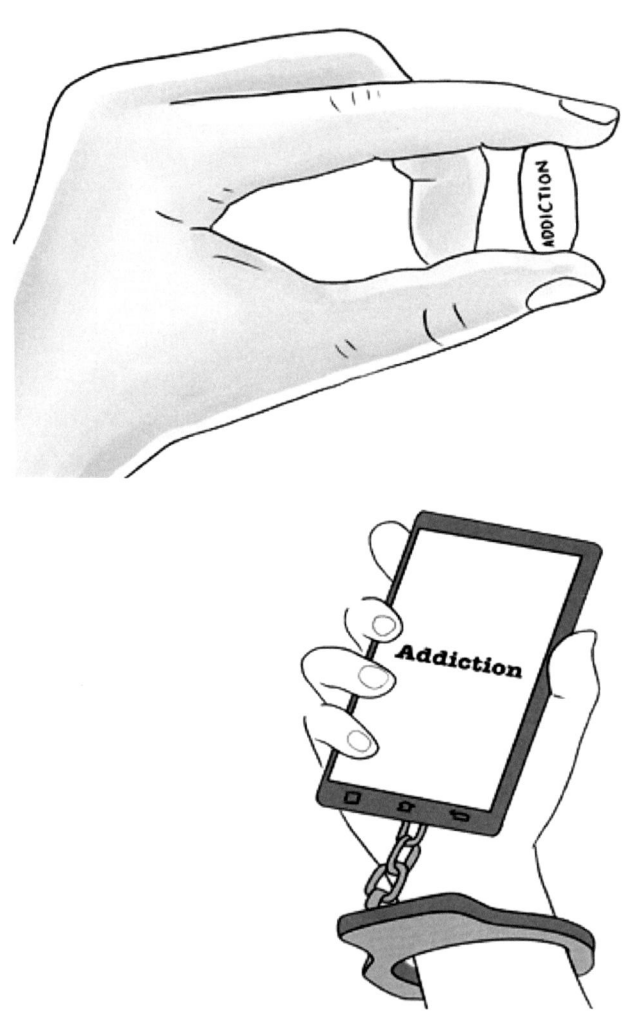

# FORTY-FOUR

**"It is more powerful to speak up, than to silently resent."
Unknown**

I am a strong believer that in some instances, silence is either consent or agreement.

I made the decision today to speak out about something that we just don't speak about enough; bullying! When I was in secondary school, people once tried to bully me. I had no control over them calling me names, and for them, their reasons for treating me that way were justified. I am a black African woman and I am proud of this, but I was once ashamed of this because people made me feel as though it was an illness to be black African. It was frowned upon to have an African accent, it was almost intolerable to have dark skin. I dreaded going to school because I had already played out how the day would go, and the thought of facing the bullying was simply exhausting.

I have never been a push-over. I knew how to stand for myself, but I just wanted to be accepted for how God decided to create me. But this was not always my experience.

I only found out the extremity of Africa's 'poverty' when I came to England. I had a good life in Africa, but the minute someone knew I was African, they looked at me with pity. I didn't understand it at first. My dad was a doctor; my mum was an English teacher at a top-rated school. It goes without saying, I had a good life. It was years later that I understood that even the smartest of people can be ignorant enough to think we all lived in huts and climbed trees (although I did climb trees, for fun and not because I was a child soldier). Even people who seem intelligent lack the common sense to consider that being black does not mean you were born into poverty by default and having an African accent does not make you illiterate. I am sure there are people of other races that have endured similar stereotypical behaviour.

In addition to being African, I also looked like my father, so strongly that I looked like a young boy. To make matters worse, I had very short hair. (I am not sure why parents do this?) Now when you take the combination of the above, I am sure you can imagine how tough some days were, because some people can be mean, weak and cowards. It is never okay to make someone else feel inferior to you because they are different. We will never have exact same beliefs, opinions or lifestyle, but this does not give anyone the right to make a person's life miserable.

If you have been bullied and you are still affected today, if you are still getting bullied now, whether at school, work or any other place. By a colleague or a boss, please do not stay silent. It is never okay for another person to be the reason why you can't do certain things or be the cause of your depression. I was never the kind of person who allowed other people's opinions of me to have a long-impact on my life. I decided to rise above it all. Furthermore, if you are witnessing someone getting bullied or being taken advantage of, please help them. If you cannot, at least find someone who might be able to.

I am extremely proud to be black, and even more proud to be African. I shout it from the rooftops because I am fearfully and wonderfully made, and I was created for a purpose. Nobody will take that away from me, especially not because of their ignorance. Additionally, let's just say I did not turn out that bad after all. I used every horrible thing that people ever said about me and made myself a better person.

Life has a way of making you reap exactly what you sow, so don't even preoccupy your mind with worries about the bullies. We need to understand that everyone is different. There are people who are still affected today by the things people said to them when they were younger. Do you know that some of those bullies have probably moved on? They probably would not even remember who you are, but here you are still paying for their ignorance. It is not worth the worry, so rise above it and be happy because life is far too short. Some of us may be friends with people who do or say bad things to people, and we witness it but choose to be silent. If this is you, you are just as bad as the people doing the bullying. Silence is you agreeing with it, especially if you have the power to do something about it.

Let's learn to speak up more because you can save a life. I say NO to bullying. It has no place in my life, not today, not tomorrow, not ever.

**PLEASE SAY SOMETHING TO SOMEONE.**

# FORTY-FIVE

魁 I 嗀

*"When you have hurt somebody, and you don't know how to start repairing the damage; saying 'I am sorry', may just be a good start."*
**Noella Kazadi**

Has there been a point in your life where you have been certain about something, but then it turns out to be wrong? How many of us actually admit when we were wrong or made mistakes? How many of us will admit how it affected other people? Would you put aside your pride and apologise for being wrong?

We live in a society where we are encouraged to have the confidence to be whoever we want and not care what other people think or feel about it. There are not enough people who are teaching us to understand that we live on this Earth with other people, and sometimes we'll need to acknowledge our mistakes. If you said or perceived something that was far from the truth and you discover you were wrong, you should have the courage and determination to apologise. You should be able to accept that you were wrong and make it known that you are trying to rectify it.

You know that when a story breaks in the media, it will be reported as though the broadcaster knew the person since the day he took his first breath. It will be all over the news and on every media outlet and repeated so much that you don't even have room to challenge this new popular belief. However, when the truth is eventually exposed, it will be reported via small print, on an advert that no one pays attention to. Some people never have the chance to restore their credibility, especially when they are innocent because the media doesn't shout-out an apology; it is whispered in a sound proof room.

Can we avoid becoming a 'social-media' society? Some people find themselves in the centre of accusations, despite being innocent. It is not weakness to admit your wrongs, it is not weakness to apologize, but it is a weakness to not fix the problems you've caused.

You will find that you have bodies around you who will encourage you to take the wrong path. If you look up, you will notice I said, 'bodies' and not 'friends' or even 'people'. Some people who we consider as friends are not our friends; they're extra bodies that can just be counted as numbers because they do not help us to do what is right. Imagine you are drinking bleach that you know will surely kill you if you continue drinking it, but you have someone there tapping your back, giving you words of encouragement to keep on drinking. They say to you, "Keep going, dear, you're nearly there."

It is not that you don't know it is bleach, nor that it will kill you, but the fact that someone is encouraging you is quite sickening. Well, that is exactly the role of certain people in our lives who encourage us to continue hurting others even when we have discovered we were very wrong. You are not just destroying that person, you are also destroying yourself.

You don't need to apologise for what you know is right, (unless you feel convinced to do so) but in other cases, if you have a conscience, you will know that you owe someone an apology and that's okay. You're human and you made a mistake. Some of us have phone calls and meet-ups to organise after reading the above. Just let them know you are sorry; it's a good start.

**NO MORE SMALL PRINT, DISCLAIMER-STYLE APOLOGY. CAPITALISE IT.**

# FORTY-SIX

❧ I ❧

*"A person who falls and gets back up, is much stronger than the person who never fell."*
*Roy T Bennett*

Have you ever had a promising start with something? You were committed, energetic and determined, yet at some point you just lost it? You fell off the rail and you don't even know how you managed to get so far from where you used to be. Well, this message is for you.

Some people stay down, not because they don't want to get back up, but they're either scared that they will fall again or that it's too late for them to get up. If this sounds like you, I think that you're wrong. I think you should fight and push. I can see that you're not satisfied with that suggestion, but you need a push, so here it is. Get up and start over. You need to understand that even though starting again is not easy, it is neither impossible.

Imagine you were in a coma for 20 years and suddenly you wake up and decide to pick up where you left off. Do you realise that it will require more than just setting your mind to start afresh? The problem is that people who are starting again set spontaneous and crazy expectations for themselves or for other people.

Here's another scenario: Take your leg and wrap it up. Don't use it for two years. Once that time has passed, remove the bandage and try to use your leg again. You will realise that your leg will not work at all, or at least not as well as before.

Now, if you were determined to walk again, you'd learn to walk again like a child who is taking their first steps. You will start holding onto items for support as you walk, then as time progresses you will gain enough body strength to walk unaided. We tend to look at the people we started with and judge them by how far they might be ahead of you, but this should never be your concern. Focus on your journey and focus on your walk. Everyone has their own battles to fight. As I have previously said, things are not always what they first appear to be. Everything you have been through will make you stronger, will make you a survivor, and above all, can be used as a stepping stone, not a covering stone. The journey is not over, you can do this.

**PICKING UP WHERE YOU LEFT OFF OR STARTING AFRESH? JUST KEEP GOING.**

# FORTY-SEVEN

*"Get to know who you are. Your strengths and weaknesses, in order to make a change. Do not use your acquired knowledge to look down on yourself."*
**Noella Kazadi**

Today I realised that there is a big difference between being self-conscious and being conscious of self. You need to be strong enough to not be so self-conscious that it becomes insecurity; however, you need to be so conscious of self to know your true value.

Ladies, most commonly in our generation we feel like if we lessen the clothes we have on and increase the make-up we wear, and the smaller our bodies are, we'll get more male attention, and this will guarantee us feelings of happiness and satisfaction. To some extent it is not our fault, because we live in a world that has become backwards. As a society, we sexualize everything, including chocolate and washing-powder. Society has created an unrealistic view of the world and how we must behave in it, and now everyone feels they must match up to its expectations. We are not entirely free of responsibility in this because we do have a choice in deciding who and what we want to be, or ought to be, and that is not up to society. The only problem is that after we have obtained all of the above, we still feel unsatisfied. We become self-conscious, and we can't step outside the door in the beautiful skin that God created us in. We can't look at ourselves in the mirror unless we are wearing expensive make-up to make us feel that we are beautiful. We can get the best grades, have the best jobs, have loving husbands and perfect home, but it will still feel as though we are not good enough. This is something we must address and overcome from within.

Gentlemen, you too can be self-conscious. Society teaches you to live beyond your means and manhood is judged by the number of women you can get. Respecting a lady is considered weakness. Society has informed you that being a man means you can never ask for help, not even when you're drowning. Once again, these are all elements of self-consciousness; it develops insecurities that take over our minds, our lives and our destinies.

Let's try this, let's make the decision to be more conscious of self. Do what makes you happy (make sure it's legal and Christ-like) and discover who you truly are again. Do what you've always wanted to do, rather than being confined by the limitations placed by society. Be so conscious of self to know you deserve better than what you have been allowing people to do to you. Be so conscious of self that you know you are not perfect and that you are still a work in progress. Whether it is the parts of your body you don't like or the areas of your life you are still improving. There are some of your so-called friends who just need to go. You can take a break from taking care of everyone else and for once take care of yourself. Being conscious of self is not about acknowledging that you are perfect, but rather seeing how imperfect you are and still loving yourself. It's about continuous growth and figuring out who you want to be today, but still working hard to be the best version of yourself tomorrow. If you decide to change your perspective, you may just spare yourself years of regret and pain. You are more powerful than you give yourself credit for. Know your true worth.

## THE CURIOUS CASE OF SELF-CONSCIOUSNESS VS BEING CONSCIOUS OF SELF.

# FORTY-EIGHT

❧ I ❧

**"Because he bends down to listen, I will pray as long as
I have breath."
Psalms 116:2**

Today will not be about me. I will be making a few prayers
for all the wonderful people that I have had the chance
to encounter in my lifetime, and those I will meet in
the future. To those who have broken me but indirectly made
me stronger, and to those who touched my heart by their
selflessness. To those that have inspired me in the biggest or
smallest way. To those that fight silent battles daily and feel that
they're alone. To the brave men and women of our time, and
those that paved the way for us to be here. To the people that
I meet daily on the street and have given me a smile, who had
no idea how much I needed it.

I make a prayer to the young girls and boys that have had to
grow up before their time, those who have been victims of
wars, famine, loss, lack of education and persecution. I am so
sorry that the world has not been fair to you. I am sorry that
you now have to step into the role of your parents for your
siblings because your parents have been taken from you. I am
sorry that your pain is not discussed on the news because of
the part of the world you were born in. Keep going, don't
give in to weakness, keep pushing forward. May our Father,
in Heaven, hear your cries and send help to you. May you live
long enough to tell your story. I know the easiest thing to do is
give up, but you cannot give your adversaries that satisfaction.

I hope that one day we will get to meet and we will remember good days together, laugh together as human beings and say a prayer together. But until then, I will be praying for you.

I make a prayer for you who are broken-hearted. I don't know who caused you so much pain, I may not even know what situation allowed you to become so bitter and depressed. You have been down for a while now, you need a hand to help you up. You need to know that someone cares. I care. I am praying for you, there is not a heart too broken for Jesus to mend. I know that prayer has become hard for you, and you feel like the whole world is crushing you down. But don't give up. I hope that we will meet one day and you can tell me about how you overcame it all. Until then, I will be praying for you.

To those who have paved the way for us, to our fathers, mothers, leaders, survivors and legends, I say a prayer for you. Thank you for the battles you fought, thank you for everything that you sacrificed to give a person like me a voice. I am grateful and praying for you.

To all the single parents, I know you're tired. I know you feel like no one understands how hard it is to raise up children alone. I want to encourage you to keep on going because you are raising kings and queens. Do not give up! Even though you will get tired, do not look at your children as burdens; they are blessings. Remember, whatever a human being is unable to fulfil or complete, God can. I am praying for you.

To you students and graduates, don't give up on your dreams because of a bad grade or because you did not get that job. I know that most of you will not admit it, but you are experiencing depression or even lost hope, and some of you are tempted to reject your dreams and settle for mediocrity. Just remember, every single person who interviews you or teaches you was once in your shoes. If they can make it, so can you. Don't lose hope, keep going. Even if you have sleepless nights or send out 100-plus job applications. Remember, good things don't come to those who wait. Good things come to those who fight and continue to believe, even when others have lost faith. I hope that we will meet one day, and you can tell me about how you finally achieved your goals. Until then I will be saying a prayer for you.

To families who are going through division and misunderstandings, who are feeling as though there is no getting past this moment of tribulation. Life is short, and once you acknowledge this, your problems won't seem so big. I am praying for unity and strength.

I am praying for those who are having suicidal thoughts. I know you feel like you have nothing left to live for, but this is not true because I know you have plenty to stay alive for. You will never know if you take your life. I know right now you feel like you will have peace if you die, but that won't be the case. Choose to live long enough to tell your story, to get better and stronger. You are much stronger than you think. I hope that when we meet you can tell me all about the battles you fought and won. For now, please remember that I am thinking of you and praying for your peace.

I make a prayer for those who are going through a season of abundance, those that have families, a home, children, husband/ wife or fiancé. To those that have found a new job, to those that have Jesus Christ in their lives, to those that have established the impossible and to those whose dreams have come true. I am praying for you to remain in that season. Remember to always count your blessings and may your abundance increase.

To those that are sick, those with a terminal illness or any type of sickness and you feel like your time to pass is near, I am praying for you to find healing. I am praying for you to find strength and to find peace. I hope that your situation can be a testimony to many people. Keep smiling, I am praying for you.

To those who are going through the impossible, overcoming it can be possible, even if you are the first. I am praying for you as you pray for me.

To the world, pray for people you love, pray for God to protect them. Pray for your leaders, that God can give them wisdom. Pray for the people who are struggling. Do not forget to also pray for yourself. We live in evil times; we need God's protection and guidance.

# IN JESUS NAME WE PRAY…AMEN…

# FORTY-NINE

華  I  华

*"We cannot stop now, the journey must
continue..."*
*Noella Kazadi*

Dear Life,

Whenever I feel like we are finally on the same page,
you surprise me with the unknown. Sometimes I am
at such a high that I cannot fathom the possibility of
having another low, and then in that moment you creep right
in and hit me right where it hurts. I feel so low that I can't
remember how I got to such a painful and confusing place. In
those times, I can't imagine how I can possibly get out of the
situation before you strike again.

I have sat through many exams in my lifetime, and when
I face any exam I feel confident in knowing what to expect.
But your procedures, dear Life, are inexorable. I have tried to
prepare myself for you, I have tried to prepare my weapons
of mass defence and attack, yet you always find a way to
surprise me with a hit that I did not train for. Can I be honest?
Sometimes I open my eyes and I wonder, *What is the point of
hoping or living when life is so unpredictable?* It is because of your
unprompted attacks that I lose motivation, and it is because of
you that I question everything. Thanks to you, I can overpower
my thoughts with a simple issue because I will be trying to
figure out the best possible way to confront it.

You have taught me unforgettable lessons. I have learnt that I can love with all my heart and not be loved back. I have learnt that I can't run away from pain because it is part of the package that comes with you. You have taught me that there is always a way, even when my mind can't even think about it. I can't forget the very important lesson you have taught me about choice, although some days I wonder who is doing the choosing; you or me? Yet, when I give in to you, you remind me that not making a choice is the same as acknowledging the power in my choice. Oh, dear Life, how art thou full of confusion and unpredictability, while the days keep coming, the hours keep multiplying and the seconds keep piling up as time passes by.

I can admit that I'm not the person I was in the beginning, when I started with you. Through the pains, struggles, laughter, sunshine and rain, we have something in common; we did not stay in the same place. I realised that you can't answer all my questions, I realised that you are limited to your function, and because of that, I live each day waiting on your next lesson.

Yours sincerely,

Mind Ltd

# FIFTY

❦ I ❦

*"You can forget my face, but remember my name.
If you forget my name; you will remember my
story."*
**Noella Kazadi**

Dear 7,

What can I tell you? What can I advise you? You're stronger than you think. You have so many unvoiced thoughts just waiting to be put into words. It's time to switch on the light and stop fearing the dark. Everyone around you seems much bigger than you, much smarter and more put-together, but remember that everything that you are going through will not end your destiny. You are here in the Motherland, enjoying the beauty of nature and the blessings of family. Understand that some of those family members will not make it. Please know that everything will not be the way you remember it now, both the good and bad, but all of it will shape you. You will stop being angry at people's inability to understand you all the time; you will see more smiles and less frowns.

You will not always be the shy girl in the background. You will step up, but it will take time. Some will encourage you, some will see it as an act, but neither of them will stop you. You will have testing times. Some points of life will test your loyalty, your perseverance and your zeal, but through all those times one thing will get stronger: your faith in God. Speaking of

God, you may not believe me, but you will become a preacher, motivational speaker, a missionary and a lawyer someday. I know you are wondering: *How would this happen? How is it even possible? I mean, look at you.* Well, life has a funny way of working out.

You will have some temporary friendships, there will be people that will come as wolves covered in sheep's clothing and you will have crocodile teeth shown at you when you least expect it. But don't worry, you will also meet people who will change your perspective on life forever. You will have great role models, as well as great life experiences which will turn you into a happy person. You will also hurt people and owe them apologies along the way. Your love for the Motherland is very important because it will bring you back with a greater purpose. Remember to always read between the lines. You will meet many people who will tell you what you can and can't achieve. You will lose jobs, time and energy, but you will learn to know what to get back and which loss to accept.

I assure you that you will eventually grow into your head, the head jokes will die down, (at least they won't affect you anymore) and then there will be something else to joke about. You will become a beautiful and motivated lady. You will be unapologetic about what you stand for, you will learn to express yourself away from anger, and you will learn to not allow fear to limit your life's potential.

You will see the world and meet people of all colour, backgrounds and beliefs, and you will be inspired by their amazing strength, perseverance and souls. You will also inspire others through the love of God, and through your own life experience. You will learn to say a few words in different languages. You will remind young people, just like you, that everything is possible, and you will assure them that with the grace of God on their side, they can do anything. You will go to schools and speak life into young girls who don't yet know their worth, and you will speak to young men about their life potential. You will make new friends from around the world.

I hope I was able to reassure you of what you can expect. I mean, this is not the full story, there are still many unwritten parts that are unknown even to me right now. Maybe we can regroup again in the next 5-10 years? Here are some tips to keep you going until then: Trust God, stay humble, give yourself permission to grow, don't respond to their opinions and above all, challenge yourself. A good challenge for you is to write a book. Don't forget to be happy along the way, inspire yourself first and once you are done with this list, go back to my first tip. Finally, to the unknown, we wait...

# A LETTER TO 7-YEAR-OLD ME.

# About the Author

Noella Kazadi best describes herself as a child of God, with a mission to fulfil her earthly calling. In the church setting, she is an ordained teacher of the gospel, established in Living Waters Church (Wolverhampton, UK). She was born in the Democratic Republic of Congo to Christian parents on the 5th of May 1993. Her father Dr Claude Kazadi is the senior pastor of Living Waters Church and a medical doctor. He later completed a PhD in the UK, which allowed him to be a Lecturer both in the UK and in Africa in Human Physiology. Her mother Sylvie Kazadi is also an ordained pastor and she was a teacher in the DRC. She later studied law in the UK, and she now works in the government sector as a minister. Noella is one of nine children, and she is the second oldest. Noella began her ministry from a very tender age in DRC, where she sang in the mass choir at the age of 7. Once she and her family relocated to the UK, she continued to sing in the choir. At the age of 12, she started interpreting for her father in church from French to English. She began to preach at the age of 14, and she later commenced her external ministry in youth conferences, crusades and TV appearances when she was 16 years old.

Noella attended Primary school at Holy Trinity Church of England. She attended secondary school, as well as Sixth Form at Our Lady and St Chads Catholic Sports College. At this stage, she began to explore her passion for a career as a lawyer. Soon after sixth form, Noella studied her undergraduate degree in LLB Law at Staffordshire University; she completed this three years later in 2014. She returned the following year to do her postgraduate studies, this was the Legal Practice Course, (LPC) to aid her on her journey of becoming a lawyer. After

Noella completed her studies, she was blessed with various legal jobs that have allowed her to enhance her career. She has several years' experience of working in private practice law firms, as well as working in the government sectors. Her areas of interest have been in Family Law, Employment Law, Commercial Litigation and a new-found passion in Mining Law. In January 2018, Noella graduated with her Master's in Law (LLM) from the University of Wolverhampton.

One thing that is dear to Noella's heart is her passion of being a philanthropist. Noella became a missionary and undertook her first crusade in 2015 in the DRC. Since then, she frequently travels to Kenya, Congo and other countries in Europe preaching the gospel of Christ Jesus. The passion to help people led Noella to start a Non-profit charity called 'Bright Destiny Organisation'. The charity has been supporting children and young adults in developing countries by sponsoring their education and giving street children the opportunity to return to school. The charity's aim in the UK is to equip young students with transferable skills which can help them succeed in their education and careers. The charity undertakes this by providing workshops, networking events, placements schemes and professional development support. The charity is in its early stages, but it is a growing vision. Find out more by visiting www.brightdestiny.co.uk or Bright Destiny Organisation on social-media.

Finally, Noella hopes that her story will inspire you to never give up. She is not a finished product, but she is still a work in progress. Noella plans to return to university to undertake a PhD which will focus on International Trade Law in the Mining Sector in the DRC.

She hopes that her story will stimulate each person to never dilute their dreams based on challenges or discouragement, the sky is not the limit; shoot for the stars. It has not been an easy journey, it has come with many obstacles, but her faith and having positive people around her have been her strength through everything. With so many other aspirations still waiting to be unveiled, there is only one question remaining: Is she married, engaged or single?

Thank you for reading.